Working Clean and Sober

D0770618

Working Clean and Sober

A Guide for All Recovering People

David Skibbins, Ph.D.

N HAZELDEN®

INFORMATION & EDUCATIONAL SERVICES

Library Resource Center
Renton Technical College
3000 NE 4th St.
Renton, WA 98056-4195

616
.8606
SKIBBEN
2000

Hazelden
Center City, Minnesota 55012–0176

1-800-328-0094
1-651-213-4590 (Fax)
www.hazelden.org

©2000 by David Skibbins
All rights reserved. Published 2000
Printed in the United States of America
No portion of this publication may be reproduced in any manner
without the written permission of the publisher

Library of Congress Cataloging-in-Publication Data
Skibbins, David, 1947–
    Working clean and sober: a guide for all recovering people/David
    Skibbins.
        p. cm.
    Includes index.
    ISBN 1-56838-551-X (pbk.)
        1. Recovering addicts—Life skills guides. 2. Recovering addicts—
    Employment—Life skills guides. I. Title

HV4998 .S59 2000
616.86'06—dc21   00–044998

Editor's note

The excerpt from pages 65–66 of *A.A. Comes of Age* and the Twelve
Steps of Alcoholics Anonymous have been adapted and reprinted
with the permission of Alcoholics Anonymous World Services, Inc.
(AAWS). Permission to use the excerpt from the book *A.A. Comes of
Age* and to reprint and adapt the Twelve Steps does not mean that
AAWS has reviewed or approved the contents of this publication, or
that AAWS necessarily agrees with the views expressed herein. AA is
a program of recovery from alcoholism *only*—use of this excerpt and
AA's Steps or an adapted version of its Steps in connection with programs and activities which are patterned after AA, but which address
other problems, or use in any other non-AA context, does not imply
otherwise.

The poem on pages 213–214 is from *Circles in the Water* by Marge
Piercy. Copyright ©1982 by Marge Piercy. Reprinted by permission of
Alfred A. Knopf, a division of Random House, Inc.

            04   03   02   01   00   6   5   4   3   2   1

Cover design by David Spohn
Interior design and typesetting by David Enyeart Design

Contents

Acknowledgments

I owe much of the material about coaching to the training I received at Coaches Training Institute (CTI) in San Rafael, California, and to the work of the founders of CTI, Henry Kimsey-House, Laura Whitworth, and Karen Kimsey-House.

I am also indebted to C. J. Hayden for her work in distinguishing between coaching and therapy and between coaching and consulting. Thanks to Lauren Powers, who taught me about "the Ladder." Thanks to David Balser, Cynthia Dyson, and Brenda Dahlie at BC Hydro and to Don Semmler of Marriott Hotels for their help with chapter 13.

My clients have been my teachers for the past twenty-five years, and I have been inspired by the clients mentioned in this book, and all the others who have enriched my life.

I could not have done this without the encouragement of Steve Lehman at Hazelden, the daily assistance of my personal copy editor Laura Kennedy, and the patience and support of my amazing agent Laurie Harper.

Finally, I am thankful for the ever-present love of my daughter, Heather, and the ongoing championing of my cherished wife, Marla.

If You Need Some Help in a Hurry

- You just picked up this book and you want to know if it's worth buying—check out the worksheets in the back (in appendix 3).
- You are still in treatment for drug and alcohol problems or you just got out—go to chapter 1.
- You just started going to Twelve Step meetings—try chapter 2.
- You are dealing with your addictions—to over- or undereating, nicotine, gambling, debting, or sex addiction issues—see chapter 11.
- Anger or resentment is tearing you up—check out chapter 4.
- You are out of a job or looking for a new job—see chapter 5.
- You have an upcoming business trip or big company party coming up, and it's making you nervous—see chapter 6.
- You are burning out at work—look at chapters 3 and 9.
- You want to see how recovery can transform management—see chapters 12 and 13
- You want to see what is coming after Capitalism—see chapter 13.

The introduction will give you a quick tour of these and the other chapters. Bon voyage.

Library Resource Center
Renton Technical College
3000 NE 4th St.
Renton, WA 98056-4195

Introduction

Congratulations! You have made the single most life-affirming decision of your life. You are in recovery. Now, if you can just keep your job!

This entire book is devoted to supporting you in being gainfully employed throughout your recovery, and throughout your life. Recovery offers some tough challenges in the workplace. It also gives us some powerful, positive perspectives for understanding our lives. We can use the emotional and ethical muscles developed in recovery to excel beyond our nonrecovering co-workers.

But first we have to keep from being fired and keep from relapsing. Not an easy process, but definitely doable.

A Tour through the Chapters

In the first section of this book, we look at what you need to survive at work during the first months in recovery. What tools do we need in that first week back from a treatment center? In chapter 1 there are essential survival tools that anyone in recovery will find useful and lifesaving. They will help you handle guilt, shame, and things that trigger your cravings and denial.

What about those of us who didn't go into a treatment center, but are doing it all with outpatient treatment or recovery group support? Chapter 2 addresses the special needs of this group.

There are some survival strategies that any recovering person needs. Chapter 3 is like a toolbox filled with tricks, plans, and schemes to derail the old addict part of your brain and support the recovering clean and sober person you now are.

Sooner or later anger comes along to challenge your recovery. In chapter 4 you'll learn how to face it and how to use the four C's (Chill, Channel, Clean the slate, and Conflict management) to release anger skillfully.

Chapter 5 looks at the problem of being out of work. The stress of leaving a job or getting fired, being jobless, and looking for work needs special attention in recovery. Chapter 6 looks at traveling and entertaining at work without threatening your sobriety.

In the second section we look at your first year of recovery and the work-related issues that come up in that tumultuous period. Chapter 7 looks at how to create healthy support.

When you say "Yes!" to recovery, to your life vision, to self-care, and to your career goals, you must also say no to other aspects of your life. In chapter 8 you will get some tools for making those hard choices and for learning to choose from passion and ideals, rather than from "shoulds."

The final section of this book looks at recovery and work issues from a wider perspective. Chapter 9 examines how we can work with the issue of burnout by using the principles we have learned in recovery. Chapter 10 gives you an opportunity to dream again. Addiction turned many of our life visions sour. In recovery we get the opportunity to re-vision our lives. Using some techniques of recovery life coaching, you will get a chance to redirect your life toward values you hold dear.

Chapter 11 applies all these principles and techniques to other addictions, such as overeating, debting, gambling, and sex addictions. Chapter 12 applies the principles of the Twelve Steps to management. And Chapter 13 paints a picture of a future workplace that fully embraces recovery values.

The first two appendixes contain resources for supporting your recovery. These include an annotated bibliography of recovery-related books and resources on the Internet for recovering folks.

Tools and Worksheets

The third appendix is a collection of workbook pages to accompany many of the tools found in this book. When a tool is mentioned in the book, it will include a reference number so that you can find the related item in the back of the book. Speed reading through this book is not very useful. Take the time to use the worksheets and do the exercises. They will help you make this book your own.

About the Stories

The stories in this book all came from my experience, first as a psychotherapist working for seventeen years with folks in recovery and then as a recovery life coach, doing personal and professional life coaching with clients, many of whom are in recovery.

The psychotherapy was done in both group and individual sessions, and the coaching happened over the telephone.

I have changed enough details in clients' stories to maintain their confidentiality and anonymity. But their words are real. They can tell you, even better than I can, what it's like inside recovery at work.

About the Author

I have been a licensed psychotherapist for twenty years. I have been in recovery for eighteen years. I have been an adjunct professor in several San Francisco Bay area universities and have taught graduate courses in addiction treatment for a decade. I have been hired, fired, and self-employed. I have managed a real estate office, started a small business, trained sales agents, consulted to businesses and nonprofit organizations, and coached recovering and nonrecovering businesspeople.

About the Use of the Phrase "Drugs and Alcohol"

Throughout this book I have used the convention of separating "drugs and alcohol" and "drinking and drug use." I am very aware that alcohol is just another psychoactive drug. However, since there are a significant number of people whose primary addiction is alcohol, I use this convention to include them in our conversation. Were I just to say "all drugs" and call drinking "drug use" (which it is), some people might not think I was referring to their addiction.

About Caffeine and Tobacco

Another position I take in this book is that the addictions of cigarette smoking and caffeine abuse don't necessarily have to be kicked in early recovery. Certainly nicotine and caffeine are both addictive, toxic psychoactive drugs. Smoking can be fatal. And I believe long-term recovery requires the person to come to terms with these substances. If the recovering person can break these addictions early, so much the better for his or her health and well-being. But I feel a little like a triage medical officer.

That's the person in a military hospital who decides who can go in for surgery and who must wait, even though waiting may prove fatal. So, too, the recovering person must determine how much he or she can endure in early recovery. It may be advisable, for example, for some people to go ahead and continue smoking for two years while they get free from other drugs and alcohol before they tackle nicotine. That would be preferable to relapsing and thinking that all recovery is bogus or just too hard. I don't want them to leave recovery and die the walking death of addiction. But since it *is* a lethal addiction in its own right, I do address smoking in chapter 11.

Many old-timers in recovery smoke and drink coffee. Newcomers judge them and say, "Well, they aren't really in recovery." Before you judge them, listen to where their lives were then and where their lives are now. I don't smoke, I don't use caffeine, and I try not to judge people who do.

PART ONE

Early Recovery

A Time of Hope and Fear

CHAPTER ONE

Your First Week Back

"How am I going to stay sober today?"

This is a bigger question than "How am I going to make it without drinking or doing drugs today?" It also includes this question: "How am I going to handle all the stress and strangeness of my life as a sober person?"

The final personal story in the Big Book of Alcoholics Anonymous speaks right to the heart of the issue of very early recovery: "God willing, we members of AA may never again have to deal with drinking, but we have to deal with sobriety every day."

Dealing with sobriety means facing a long string of challenges. One of the hardest is facing that first day back at work. It seems endless. This chapter will take you through that first week. In it, you will find lifesaving tools to help you survive sobriety. The five tools in this chapter are designed specifically for that first week back in the world.

Let's take a look at the first week through the eyes of a client of mine, someone who barely made it through this difficult time:

Frank's Story

Frank started therapy with me right after coming out of treatment. He was a tall, quiet man, but behind his mask was a store of resentment, which he kept well hidden from the outside world. It threatened his recovery in those early days.

"After twenty-one days, I got out of my addiction treatment program. I went back to my old job as an accountant. At first, everyone was very friendly and polite in welcoming me back. But they had changed. Now, every time I called in sick, there was this suspicion in their voice.

"I told a few of them that I was having a hard time. They seemed annoyed. One guy said, 'What's the matter with you? Drugs ruined your life. Just quit, and never go back. What's so hard about that?'

"I stopped talking about it to anyone at work. I started hating work. It got so that every morning I was thinking about going to see my dealer instead of going back to work in a place where everyone was waiting for me to fail."

Frank is clean and sober today, but he still remembers the fear and isolation he faced in his first week back. His is a common story. Some clients have shared with me stories of co-workers who made their transition a celebration, rather than an ordeal. But you will often find resentment or negativity greeting you in your return to work. Frank's story can teach you about five challenges that must be faced and overcome.

Challenge #1: Distrust

The first challenge you will face is suspicious co-workers and supervisors. Frank speaks right to the heart of that issue. When you have a distrustful co-worker confronting a shaky, testy, newly recovering addict, it can be like two rams butting heads—a lot of noise, a lot of drama, and not much progress. So let's separate the wildlife and look at each perspective separately.

Wild Animal #1: Your Co-worker. The suspicious co-worker usually comes at you with a history of frustration and disappointment. Part of this history has to do with your actions when you were using and drinking.

Keep in mind, co-workers had to endure the effects of your prerecovery behavior. Do you know what they might remember best about you? Maybe it's the unexplained absences, the missing funds, the forgotten deadlines, your depression, and your negativity. Why should they trust you again? Co-workers are afraid to hope. They are afraid of being disappointed once again.

Co-workers also bring along their own emotional baggage. They have collected addiction-related resentment from long before they ever met you. They have been wounded by other alcoholics and by other self-centered insensitive junkies. All those past letdowns and discontents build up a head of steam, which can explode in suspiciousness. So you, as a former addict, face more than just your own mistakes. In addition, you remind your co-workers of some distasteful people you have never met. That's why this challenge is so hard.

Wild Animal #2: You. The other wild animal in this interaction is you. Does this inner conversation sound familiar? "Why are they so suspicious of me? After all, I am the one who is doing the hard work. Let them spend a month in treatment and see how they would feel! Here I am working so damn hard to save my life, and all they give me is their resentment and their garbage."

No one is ever quite as righteous as a newly recovering addict. You feel as though you deserve some appreciation for the incredible sacrifice you're making by giving up your chemical crutches. When people don't trust you, it's like someone kicking you when you're down.

What you don't see too well is that deep inside, you don't really trust yourself. In that first week, the temptation to drink or use is so huge, and your will so shaky! Everything is touch and go. When you encounter other people's distrust, it activates your own doubts. You vigorously insist on your trustworthiness, hoping to convince both them and yourself.

Convincing yourself is really the hard part. You face a fearful adversary: your own Inner Judge. He or she is a hanging judge and has already tried and convicted you. The reading of this Judge's sentence can take years. "You did this wrong, you did that wrong," and on and on. Life in the courtroom of your mind is very stressful. We will learn how to silence the Judge later on in the book, but right now let's learn how to turn down the overall stress level that exists inside you and around you. What can you do to lower the tension in this pressure cooker?

Tool #1: Two Times Five Equals AOK (Worksheet 1–1)

Relax. You don't have to figure all this stuff out. Actually, don't take this the wrong way, but you are too clouded right now to be clear about what is your stuff and what is your co-worker's stuff. The clouds will start clearing in a few months. Then you will know more about what's going on.

In very early recovery, all you need to do is *keep it really simple*. So here is Simple Instruction #1: Make *two* support calls *every day* while at work. Not big complicated calls. Not long protracted calls. Simple calls. Calls *one to five* minutes long. Just connect in the morning and in the afternoon with a sponsor, or a friend, or anyone who is just a little saner than you. If you are running into distrust at work, talk about it. That will help release it.

If you get an answering machine, just leave a message: "Hi, it's me, David. Just wanted to call and check in today. My boss is still being a pain, but I can handle it. Bye." I recommend a total of two to ten minutes each day. Do this every workday for the first month. Let someone in to help you.

Challenge #2: Denial

In this challenge, you take a look at the mother of all defenses, denial.

When you don't want to face something, you push it away. As a kid, you might have tried to hide the broccoli under a napkin or sneak liver to the dog under the table. You (and every other human being) do sneaky things like that *every day* in your mind. Often, you do it so secretly that *even you* don't notice it. For instance, people may have told you for years that you had some sort of drinking or drug problem. But you conveniently and quickly forgot their feedback. That is denial.

Treatment hammers away at the walls of denial, helping you see the extent of your problem. Typically, you fight it all the way, minimizing, avoiding, wiggling, and trying to escape. Finally you give up and look squarely at the mess you've made of your life. You get past *some* of your denial. Every year in recovery removes another layer of denial.

Don't worry, you don't have to get rid of all your denial

on your first day back at work. However, there is a particular brand of denial that needs to be looked at right away
in your recovery, to help you survive work.

Recovery makes you sick. While you were getting in
training to be a party animal, your body had to adjust to
regular dosages of strong chemicals. Finally, it succeeded.
You became physically comfortable in your addiction. For
your body, being dosed became the norm. In recovery, you
are radically altering your internal environment. You are
taking away the chemicals your body has come to love and
need. Your poor body has a whole new norm to get used
to. It fights back!

And you feel sick, all different kinds of sick. Sometimes
it feels like the flu. Sometimes it is this itchy irritability
that makes you want to go out and shoot strangers on the
street for fun. Sometimes it is exactly like a hangover.
Sometimes you feel stupid, like you lost thirty points of
IQ somewhere. And often it is this vast weakness and
bone-deep exhaustion. You feel like you can barely move.

The problem with all these miserable symptoms is that
they make you want to stay home from work. Unfortunately, you bring a long ignoble history to the act of calling in sick. As Frank put it, "Now, every time I called in
sick, there was this suspicion in their voice."

So you decide to hide your bone-deep weariness. You
want to convince everyone that everything is a piece of
cake. You are fine, fine, fine. Recovery is no big deal. For
the folks who don't know you have an addiction, you really want to create the impression that you are OK.

All of which is a total crock. Some days, just getting
dressed is a major victory. You can barely remember how
you got to work this morning, let alone play full out as a
team leader. On a good day, you operate at about 15 percent efficiency.

So you go into denial. "This is not really happening to me. Actually, I am just fine. Go ahead and pile on the work, I can handle it. Maybe I need even more of a workload!" You try to power through. You do a lot of "image management," keeping the mask intact in spite of the mess who is behind it.

Then you crash and burn because your body gives out on you. Or maybe it doesn't give out. It just aches silently. Either way, you are headed for Grim Recovery. This is a land where everything looks gray and miserable, joyless and depressed. The addict inside you is always glad to see sobriety associated with misery. "Keep that up!" says your inner alcoholic. Soon, it will be able to convince you that using drugs and alcohol is the only way to bring a little fun back into your miserable life.

You may also be headed for a stress-related illness or accident. In 1967 two researchers, Thomas H. Holmes and Richard H. Rahe, created a do-it-yourself stress test. By adding the Life Change Units (LCUs) values of the past year, you can predict the likelihood of stress-related illness or accident. I added in the recovery and addiction scores based on my clinical experience. (See worksheet 1–2.)

The Holmes and Rahe Stress Test

Life Changes: Add up the score of the changes that have happened to you in the past year.

___ Death of a spouse: 100

___ Divorce: 73

___ Relapse from recovery: 67

___ Marital separation: 65

___ Detention in jail or institution: 63

___ Death of a close family member: 63

___ Addictive behavior: 60

___ Major personal injury or illness: 53

___ Marriage: 50

___ Going into recovery: 48

___ Being fired at work: 47

___ Marital reconciliation: 45

___ Retirement: 45

___ Major change in health or behavior of a family member: . 44

___ Pregnancy: 40

___ Sexual difficulty: 40

___ Gaining a new family member through birth,
adoption, or remarriage: 39

___ Major business readjustments: 39

___ Major change in financial state: 38

___ Death of a close friend: 37

___ Change to a different line of work: 36

___ Major increase in fights with spouse: 35

___ Taking on a mortgage: 31

___ Foreclosure on a mortgage or loan: 30

___ Major change in responsibility at work: 29

___ Son or daughter leaving home: 29

___ In-law troubles: 29

___ Outstanding personal achievement: 28

___ Spouse begins to cease work outside of home: 26

___ Going back to school: 26

___ Major change in living condition (rebuilding, remodeling): 25

___ Revision of personal habits: 24

___ Troubles with superior, boss: 23

___ Major change in working hours, conditions: 20

___ Change in residence: 20

___ Change to a new school: 20

___ Major change in usual type and/or amount of recreation: 19

___ Major change in church activities: 19

___ Major change in social activities: 18

___ Purchasing a new car, or other big purchase: 17
___ Major change in sleeping habits: 16
___ Major change in number of family get-togethers: 15
___ Major change in eating habits: 15
___ Vacation: 13
___ Christmas or holiday observance: 12
___ Minor violations of the law: 11

Add up your total Life Change Units (your LCUs).
Total LCU below 150: . . . . 35 percent chance of illness or
accident within two years
Total LCU between 150 and 300: 51 percent chance of illness or
accident
Total LCU over 300: . . . . 80 percent chance of illness or
accident

Pretty scary, isn't it? Addiction raises stress levels, and recovery raises them again. And relapse raises them even more. The good news is that ultimately recovery lowers stress. The tough reality is that, right now, you need to take particular care of yourself.

Tool #2: On Thursday, Get the Flu!

It is time to schedule in your next illness. Co-workers do not get the concept that recovery is physically debilitating. What they do understand is the flu. Everyone gets it, and everyone needs to get away from the office to cure it. I am sure you have had "the flu" many times. Sometimes when you were high, or other times when you were too wiped out to work. That was the Hangover Flu.

This is the Recovery Flu. When you have the Recovery Flu you don't lie in bed, wallowing in self-pity, feeling

Library Resource Center
Renton Technical College
3000 NE 4th St.
Renton, WA 98056-4195

alone, sad, and sorry for your plight as an unloved recovering drunk. Isolation will not nourish you. Crawl out of the bedroom.

This is a great time to go to four meetings in one day, or spend a chunk of time with your sponsor, or walk in nature. Stay recovery-oriented, nap a lot, talk to friends, eat healthy food, and take the time to nurture yourself. Make recovery worth it.

When you come back to work on Monday, let everyone know that you are still fighting off the bug and you feel under the weather. That will explain some of your shakiness, irritability, and stupidity. This is not a lie. The bug that is fighting its way out of your system is called "addiction," and the weather you are under is one huge cloud of physical exhaustion and emotional overload.

Challenge #3: Paranoia

I'm not saying you're crazy or that you think there are listening devices in your breakfast cereal. I am talking about common, garden-variety paranoia.

We are dealing with the father of all defenses, projection. Paranoia is built on a foundation of projection. Down underneath our level of ordinary awareness, your very clever mind has learned how to defuse uncomfortable experiences. It spits them out, projecting them on others.

For instance, you might be very angry with someone you love. But you fear that if you let your anger out, this person might leave you. You can try denial for a while. Just put on a big smile and really believe you are happy to see that person. But eventually, the anger starts scratching at the door of your awareness, trying to get out. So you do the next best thing. Whatever emotion you can't stand in yourself, you paint on your beloved's face. You indignantly ask, "Honey, why are you getting so pissed with me?" You are convinced that the anger is out there, and you "know" that it's coming toward you. You get to play the innocent victim. Your "honey" just became the enemy!

Negative projection is the most harmful defense. It transforms people into dangerous foes who must be defended against or destroyed. It turns love into distrust and hate. It devastates the open heart.

Here are some common projections that come up in the mind of someone newly clean and sober.

What you feel		What you project
"I am so ashamed of what I have done."	becomes	"They judge me!"
"I am angry because I have to quit using."	becomes	"You're mad at me!"
"Can I stay sober?"	becomes	"They are waiting for me to fail!"
"I am scared every day."	becomes	"They are afraid of me losing it!"

Projection happens when you put your unacknowledged emotions onto another person. Sometimes your projections are accurate. You have read the bumper sticker, "Just because you're paranoid doesn't mean they aren't out to get you." But sometimes, you are way off base. By the time you realize it, you have so annoyed the other *person* that now they *are* ready to kill you.

Figuring out what is real and what is projection is the work of a lifetime. It is certainly way beyond the capacity of a recently dried-out brain. So that's why you have the next tool.

Tool #3: S.T.O.P. (Worksheet 1–3)

This magic phrase will help you manage your projections and deal with your co-worker's projections. It stands for Stop Talking! Obviously Projecting!

One thing that I learned while working in mental institutions is what a total waste of time it is to enter into a conversation with a projecting, suspicious, paranoid patient. I could never shake their insane convictions. I only ended up frustrating myself and creating mistrust in the mind of my patient. Instead, I learned to smile and be silent as they told me about the international conspiracy to poison radio waves.

You can spot garden-variety projection by feeling the intensity of the emotional reactions of other people. If they start screaming at you for accidentally picking up their lunch box or stealing paper clips off the top of their desk, odds are they are lost in projection. Here is what you do: (1) smile; (2) Stop Talking—*they are* Obviously Projecting; (3) apologize; and (4) get out of Dodge. You are in no condition to do anything more subtle than that.

And then there are those days when you are utterly convinced that your co-worker really took those paper clips off your desk to get back at you for all the things you've done to her. As you are rearing up to let her have it once and for all, you remember, "Stop Talking—*I am* Obviously Projecting." Smile, and create some real distance between the two of you in a hurry. Quickly, before you really blow it.

I can hear your inner voice of indignation already: "Wait a minute! You mean just walk away from every confrontation? That's not fair! What about when I am right? I'm not about to become some doormat that anyone can walk all over. I get to speak my truth!"

You have a point. It's not good to be a doormat that everyone walks all over. And, as time and sobriety go on, you will get the tools to skillfully defend yourself. But it's a little too soon for that. The first week is about survival. And fights, angry confrontations, raised voices, and hurt feelings work against survival. The junkie inside you is constantly gathering evidence about why recovery doesn't work. A few dramatic scenes are all the munitions it needs to sink your ship. So, for today, just Stop Talking and walk away. Your turn will come in a few months, when you are ready for it. Chapter 4 is all about managing anger. Let's just get through the first few days.

Challenge #4: Guilt and Shame

Congratulations! You don't have to deal with guilt and shame this week! You get a break.

Downstream from today you will have to go in and clean out the attic in your mind. When you do that, you will find footlockers full of guilt, shame, embarrassment, regret, remorse, and other messy stuff. But it is not spring cleaning this week! This week is all about survival in recovery. It is about keeping your job and making it to meetings. It is not about throwing yourself into some heavy-duty, cleansing, therapeutic process. Therefore, when incidents come up that threaten to bog you down in guilt and shame, you get to use Tool #4.

Tool #4: Vacation

No, you are not heading off to the beach for a month. Sorry. Only a little part of you is leaving town. The part we call the Inner Judge. The Inner Judge is that voice inside you that is always critical, never satisfied, and often just plain mean. It calls you names you would never let someone outside of you get away with. Names like, "stupid, fat, dumb, clumsy, ugly, idiot, drunk, crazy, doper, loser."

The job of the Inner Judge is to make you feel rotten about yourself. It hopes that, if you feel crummy enough, you might eventually make something out of your worthless life. It has no mercy and no compassion.

Eventually, you will learn how to manage that Inner Judge voice so that it stops making your life so miserable. Eventually, you may even notice how the Inner Judge teams up with the Inner Junkie to keep you addicted. (Another tool for working with the Inner Judge can be found on pages 166–167.) But for right now, you just have to send it packing. Send it on a month-long cruise, while you stay here and live your recovery. Any attack, any insult, any assault from that Inner Judge voice is a direct threat to your recovery. For now, get rid of it.

When that voice says, "You could have done that better," tell it, "Get lost and leave me alone!" When it says, "You are blowing your recovery," tell it, "Take a long hike off a short pier." Ignore anything it throws at you. It is cunning, baffling, and powerful.

Refuse to listen. Stick your fingers in your inner ears. Take a shower, take a walk, call your sponsor, do anything other than argue with it or engage it. It is very important that you not get mired down in long inner conversations filled with self-hate and self-recrimination.

The Inner Judge wins every argument because it is irrational, stubborn, and always fights dirty. So cast it out. Someday, working the Steps will teach you how to live with your past. You will accept that the mistakes you made actually can teach you how to make better future plans. All the old unresolved issues will eventually find resolution. But not this week! In six months, maybe, but not this week. For right now, kick that critical voice out the back door.

Challenge #5: Triggers

Work is a dangerous place. I don't mean jobsite health and safety issues; I mean work is a danger to recovery—the ultimate health and safety issue!

Most of your co-workers use drugs and alcohol recreationally. Many of them use chemicals addictively. Your recovery can threaten their peace of mind. They would appreciate it if you would just go back to using. Then they can relax. So they'll do what they can to get you off the wagon. They're not evil. They're just scared that, if you recover, they might have to face their drinking and drug use problems. Instead, they will invite you out to party. Strike one!

Strike two! You actually have two strikes against you. One is your addicted co-workers. The second is your old habits. If your dealer's house or favorite liquor store is on your way home, the car will steer toward it as though it had a mind of its own.

Change your route home. Drive home with a non-drinker. Interfere with your drinking and drug-related habits. If your dealer or package store home delivers, tape the number of your sponsor and AA or NA hotline on the receiver. Put recovery between you and your old habits.

There will be more on this strategy in chapter 3. For now, interrupt bad habits.

The worst habit you will face is self-hatred. This is a habit of negative thinking that plagues everyone. Most people just let that voice beat them up. This week, you can't afford that. The Inner Judge embodies self-hatred. You must ask it, not very politely, to get lost.

Two strikes don't mean that you're out. They mean you have to be really present for every activity in your life, every pitch life throws at you. You need to avoid trouble ahead of time, instead of figuring out how to get out of the mess that you just stepped in. But how do you know which path is headed toward trouble?

Tool #5: The Four Directions (Worksheet 1–4)

Here is a tool for avoiding a lot of trouble. This tool is a simple test. Use it to see if what you are doing, or what you are thinking, will serve your recovery. Don't do anything that's not on this list:

Direction #1—Stay clean and sober. Go to meetings; call therapists, sponsors, coaches, and suicide prevention hotlines; call anyone for help instead of going back to drinking or drugging.

Direction #2—Survive. Sleep as best as you can, eat as best as you can, and take at least one slow walk a day, if you can.

Direction #3—Try to physically show up on your job. Forget showing up intellectually or energetically—that will come in time. Just try to get your body there.

Direction #4—Go back to direction #1.

When your "friends" ask you to party with them, consult this list. Notice that the word "party" does not appear on this list. When you start planning to buy some drugs or booze, first consult this list. Reread direction #1. When your mind throws memories at you that you would rather forget or creates feelings that make you feel small and slimy, go back to this list. (Hint: call anyone!) When someone in your life confronts you with incidents you would rather forget, or maybe incidents you don't even remember, go back to this list. Do S.T.O.P. with whoever is confronting you. Smile, and get physically away from them. Then try direction #1.

This week, if it is not direction #1, 2, 3, or 4, avoid it.

Conclusion

Believe it or not, the first week is not the hardest week in recovery. But it is plenty hard. And it sure can feel embarrassing and awkward. Remember, this week is only seven days long. Each day ends, and it makes room for a better one. Here is your survival checklist:

- Get lots of help.
- Avoid slippery places.
- Keep your distance from angry and critical people.
- That includes you.
- Remember to call someone supportive twice a day.
- Get the flu.
- S.T.O.P.
- Send your Inner Judge on vacation.
- Follow the Four Directions.

You will make it! And, at the end of your first month,

you will have laid down solid tracks toward a new life. Let's let Frank end this chapter:

"I hated work that first week. Well, I hated me, and that spilled over to work. I really thought they all were fed up with me. But a few weeks later, things started to clear. I wasn't crawling out of bed every day, like I was eighty years old. Some days, I almost felt normal. Work sure looked a lot better after that. Funny thing, my co-workers stopped acting like monsters, too."

CHAPTER TWO

I Didn't Go to Treatment, I Just Started AA/NA

 Carl's Story

Carl was one of my coaching clients. He came into coaching after five years in recovery. He had been a loner his whole life, until discovering that he couldn't stay sober alone. His story of his first year reminded me of the power of the program to change lives.

"I never needed friends. At work, I had acquaintances. At home, I had TV and a bottle. Only it became a couple of bottles. And too many mornings when all I could do was keep on drinking. I finally realized that I was getting out of control. I was missing work so much I was in danger of losing my job.

"I couldn't afford a month in a treatment center. I was so broke I couldn't even go to a psychiatrist. My health plan didn't cover a cold, let alone treatment.

"All I could do is start going to AA. After work I'd go to a meeting. I couldn't speak, but at least I was able to sit there for an hour and not bolt out the door. After that, I'd go home, watch TV, and try to not want a beer.

"After my first relapse, I wised up. I started talking in

those meetings. And one night I recognized one of the guys there from work. A few days later he came over to my desk to say hi. We agreed to eat lunch together.

"We knew a secret about each other, and somehow that helped bring us together. Hell, going to meetings, we came to know a lot of secrets about each other. He has become my best friend. It's been two years of lunches together. We have seen each other through his first relapse, and my second (and last!) relapse.

"It makes work a pretty friendly place. We have pulled together an AA meeting at 5:30 P.M., around the corner from work. Familiar faces come wandering in. Now we have about seven of us who work together and are recovering together."

There are many paths to recovery. Some folks recover going to Hazelden or the Betty Ford Center, others by going to the corner AA or NA meeting. If the path leads to sobriety, it's the right one for you.

There are advantages to taking a month off work to go into treatment. You can let the physical reactions to recovery sweep through your body without having to call in sick. You can begin to reprogram some old addictive beliefs. And you're in a drug- and alcohol-free environment.

Doing it on your own—that is, in the fellowship of AA or NA or in therapeutic relationships, but without treatment—is a rougher road, but one many of us have walked. These days there are outpatient support groups, therapists, and addiction counselors who have extensive experience in recovery support and relapse prevention, and there are the anonymous groups.

Some of us don't go into treatment and recover by using only the Twelve Step programs. Within these groups there is a collective wisdom and understanding that is all the support many people need to stay on the road of sobriety. In parts of southern California recovery is chic, and some people go to meetings not because they are in recovery, but to see if they can spot movie stars. In the rest of the world, we just go to meetings to save our lives.

Early Recovery

Going straight into recovery while working places a major strain on your body and on your coping capacity. Expect to be working at 20 percent of your usual level. Be willing to use Tool #2, The Recovery Flu, from the previous chapter regularly. Your days may look like this: morning meeting, go to work, noon meeting, back to work, evening meeting, go home, collapse in bed. Don't think about it too much; this routine will change over time. The first ninety days are the roughest.

Looking at the Twelve Steps from the perspective of a recovery treatment therapist, I can see how brilliantly they were constructed. They address the needs of the recovering person, but beyond that they address basic human needs we all possess. Everyone wants to accept himself or herself. Everyone wants to get along well with others. We all want a lifestyle that works, and we want a context for our life that is larger than just living from day to day. We all want to make a difference in this world.

In the first few weeks you may be a lot more worried about how to make it from hour to hour without using. Thinking about the larger context for your life may be a few weeks or months off. That is why the Twelve Steps start with helping you manage cravings. Step by Step, as you are ready to take them, the Steps keep moving you to a larger and larger perspective on your life.

Like recovery itself, working the Twelve Steps naturally

divides into three phases. In phase 1, early recovery, the focus is on day-to-day survival. In phase 2, interpersonal recovery, the focus is on building self-esteem and social skills to manage the complexity of adult human interaction. Chapter 7, "Creating Support," will explore the connection between the Twelve Steps and this phase of recovery. Phase 3 is centered on making recovery the centerpiece of a meaningful life. Chapter 12 will look at how Steps Ten, Eleven, and Twelve relate to long-term recovery and work success (The Steps printed on the following pages are an adaptation. The original Twelve Steps of Alcoholics Anonymous are printed on page 265).

Phase 1 recovery is focused on managing your cravings in a way that does not lead to relapse. Steps One, Two, and Three begin with an elegant paradox that stops you from trying to manage recovery in the same way you have tried to manage abstinence or controlled usage.

Step One. We admitted we were powerless over drugs and alcohol—that our lives had become unmanageable.

Step Two. Came to believe that a Power greater than ourselves could restore us to sanity.

Step Three. Made a decision to turn our will and our lives over to the care of God *as we understood God.*

In the next chapter, "Your Relapse Prevention Tool Kit," we will take a microscope and a scalpel and dissect cravings to discover how to deflate them. In this chapter we will look at the whole issue of what it means to *manage* your cravings.

In our many attempts to control our drinking/drugging or in trying to maintain abstinence, we attempted drastic forms of management. We poured countless bottles down the drain, flushed many more drugs down the toilet, and made dramatic promises of a new beginning. We tried all sorts of approaches: permissive management, autocratic management. Nothing worked.

The first three Steps recommend a very different tactic. They ask us to face the reality that nothing you can come up with will work. That used to be a great excuse to go off on a binge. We are hopeless addicts, and we might as well enjoy it. But now the Steps suggest that facing that truth is the foundation of recovery. What a contradiction!

But there is a huge sigh of relief when we finally grasp that we will never be able to control the uprising of our cravings. After seventeen years living clean and sober I am still surprised at how strong my cravings can be at times. Recovery has nothing to do with being craving free. Some recovering people report the complete cessation of cravings. But there are plenty of us old-timers who still get the urge.

Stifling cravings through willpower did not work. The First Step strips away any attempt to pretend otherwise. Instead the addicts in early recovery are asked to turn to an authority outside of their own battered egos. This can be a sponsor, a therapist, a meeting, a church, a fellowship, some sort of divine guidance, or more likely some combination of these. Let someone or something else make decisions for a while, and you just stay sober, and keep coming back.

The management skill asked for by the Steps is surrender. In chapter 12, "The Twelve Steps for Managers and Leaders," we will look at how Twelve Step principles apply to actual management. Here we are looking at surrender as a key skill for succeeding, both in recovery and at work.

Surrender at Work

Surrender as a management skill? I know that sounds ridiculous. After all, to manage means "to control the movement or behavior" of someone. Management is all about control, power, and authority, right? Not any more.

Modern research in effective management is uncovering the reality that the most effective managers in the modern workplace govern by cooperation, influence, suggestion, and empowerment, rather than by force. Authoritarian managers pay the prices of decreased production, increased employee sick leave, accidents, and turnover. In effect, new managers need to surrender to the needs of their employees, the needs of the business, and the needs of the marketplace. Through being open to all these influences, they guide their people most skillfully on the path to results.

How does surrender at work operate? You are learning through the first three Steps what it means in recovery. When you surrender control of your addictive behavior, you allow your Higher Power to guide you. That comes in the form of timely advice from others, amazing coincidences that occur to stop you from relapsing, and intuitive guidance from a voice deep within you, which you had never listened to before. The following three phrases will help you bridge the connection between what you are learning in recovery and its application at work (see worksheet 2–1).

Let them help: Use the muscles you are developing in recovery to guide you at work. Give up having to be the expert. Learn how to ask others for their ideas about how to make something work more effectively. Ask for help. Solicit advice from everyone, customers included.

Asking for help is not just about seeking advice. You also

need to learn how to turn work over to others. It is always easier at first just to "do it yourself." You have the experience that a novice does not have. Prior to recovery you might have gotten impatient, grabbed the work out of another's hands, and grumbled, "It's easier if you just leave that to me!"

But by being patient, letting less experienced people make some mistakes, and allowing them to do a less than perfect job at first, you can get a big payoff in the future. By teaching them, you empower them and reduce your own workload.

Red light, green light: Pay attention to meaningful coincidences at work, and accept that they may be pointing you in a particular direction. If a project or task is moving forward effortlessly, that may be a signal that it is in accordance with the unfolding of the universe. If something is continually crashing and burning, it is also a signal, probably that something is out of balance. In early recovery I applied for sixteen teaching positions. After sixteen rejections I finally realized that I wasn't meant to be a college professor. I was a little thick, but finally I paid attention to the signals. I realized my Higher Power wanted me to do something else.

Calling upstairs: Listening for guidance from the voice of your Higher Power is tricky business. When it works, it is magical. When you confuse your Higher Power's voice with the voice of your Inner Addict or your Inner Judge, messes can result. So how can you tell the difference?

Listening to your Higher Power's voice is not like thinking or feeling your way around an issue. Those are great things to do, too, but information from your Higher Power is more like a knowing. The way becomes clearer and we naturally sense the right thing to do.

Sometimes the information does not come in words; it comes in a warmth, or a relaxation, or a sense of space opening up inside. Listen with your whole body. Here are three approaches for gaining closer contact with that knowing:

1. Space in your day. Sometimes inner wisdom speaks in such a soft voice that we can barely hear it. Part of the work of recovery is creating space in your day when you can be quiet enough to listen to its whisperings. You need some privacy and some quiet. You must consciously carve out a little time for this; for example, by sitting still and silent for five minutes in the morning, or taking a slow, solitary lunchtime walk or an after-dinner stroll, or simply reflecting on your day before falling asleep.

2. Knowing what to ask for. When you have created these times in your day when you can listen to the voice within, be willing to ask for all kinds of help. This is not just time for questions and issues about recovery. You are accessing a vast ocean of knowledge and wisdom. Ask about your boss, about that order from Chicago, about the date you went on last night, and about how to get through the grocery store and avoid the wine, beer, and liquor aisle. Become willing to ask for help for anything and everything. And be content with what you get.

Often it will be no answer at all. That is an answer, too. Remember those fortune-telling balls, the ones you turn over and an answer floats up to the window? "Reply hazy, try again" was one of my favorites. It requires real patience to wait for clarity. That is part of the practice of recovery.

3. Is it real or is it Memorex? Unfortunately, our Higher

Power is not the only voice we hear inside us. There are the merciless judgments of the Inner Judge. Mixed in with those are the incessant urgings of the Inner Addict, such as, "Let's go out and have some fun!" And topping off the chorus are all the relevant and irrelevant thoughts and feelings that come bubbling up from your mind in an unending stream.

Just to make things a little more difficult, any one of these voices is more than willing to disguise itself as your Higher Power and tell you that it has the answer. Here are three hints to help you sort through the static.

- Sense your body. If you feel muscles in your stomach or chest, or anywhere in your body contracting, hardening, or getting anxious, ask yourself if this is really a message from your Higher Power. Generally (although not always) there is a feeling of relaxation that comes with true intuition.

- Listen to the message. Your Higher Power sees you as naturally resourceful, wise, creative, and whole. Its guidance supports your health and well-being. If the message is harsh, judgmental, or subtly implies that you are deficient, stupid, stuck, or a mess, then begin to wonder if it might be an impostor.

- Don't blindly trust just any inner voice. You may get a dazzling insight, with a huge relaxation, and a deep inner knowing that this is the truth. And that insight might be saying, "Now you can recreationally use alcohol and other drugs!" Sit still with any message, and see if it fits into the way you want to live your life. Many of us in early recovery have gotten great ideas to quit our jobs, dump our partners, reject our parents, and head off to Alaska. Some of those ideas may, in the long run, turn out to be OK. Some may be the fast lane to disaster.

The grander the plan, the longer you need to just
sit with it and see if it looks that good a week or a
month from now. True guidance will endure.

Going from addiction to recovery can be done just by
using the support of the program. It requires that you take
very compassionate and nurturing care of yourself
through early recovery. And go to a couple of meetings a
day. You are breaking up huge, rigid patterns of behavior,
not just about addictions, but about how you are in the
world. The gift is priceless. Your life.

CHAPTER THREE

Your Relapse Prevention Tool Kit

Good cooks buy quality knives and pans. A master carpenter takes exceptional care of her or his power tools. A great violinist can spend hundreds of thousands on the perfect violin.

You are crafting your recovery. It is part science and part imaginative artistry. Your life is the performance. Your tools need precision.

Before I introduce you to the five tools in this kit, I want you to meet Sara. She became a client of mine after her first year in recovery. She sought me out because she had heard about these tools. She personally field-tested some of them, and can attest to their effectiveness.

 ### Sara's Story

Sara walked into my office dressed in a navy blue suit, nylons, and a lovely blue and gray silk scarf. She was a corporate recruiter. The holes in her ears, nose, and tongue had healed and closed. But in her first year of recovery she was a punk rocker, with hair spiked, jeans ripped, and many body parts pierced.

"I landed a sound job on the road for a struggling heavy

metal band. Being on the road meant many hours of boring travel, knocking off a few beers an hour while doing nothing. This was followed by several hours of incredibly intense work, usually on coke. Get the monitor mix right so the band can hear themselves, get the PA mix right, baby our two antique sound boards, track down feedback, and if I got it wrong, all hell broke loose. The night never ended. We went from the gig to intense partying from midnight to four in the morning. Sleep was an elective.

"There was no way I could have gotten straight in that world. But the band went clean and sober. A clean and sober metal band. That's a small niche! That meant I had to clean up and follow suit, if I wanted to stay with them.

"Thank God. It saved my life. We started going to meetings together. You haven't lived until you watch the faces around the table as ten tattooed, pierced, and spiked freaks wearing their leathers walk into a noon meeting in Sioux Falls. It's a great fellowship. Nobody ever tossed us out!

"I saw your Recovery Tool Kit posted on a bulletin board on the Web. I downloaded it and passed it out to the band. It really helped out. We were all in early recovery, and really shaky. We were just lucky that our lead guitarist never slipped. He kind of held us together as we stumbled from relapse to relapse. We all were headed toward recovery, desperately trying to put some solid time in between the slips."

When people open a first aid kit, they want exactly what they need, and they want it in a hurry. The same is true of this recovery kit. There are not a lot of superfluous syringes or surgical operating tools in here, just five tools to apply directly to your cravings and your stress.

There is also room in this kit for the tools you have already picked up. You can add tried-and-true tools you learned in treatment or at meetings, like H.A.L.T. (don't get too Hungry, Angry, Lonely, or Tired) or K.I.S.S. (Keep It Simple, Stupid). You can add tools from this book, like the first tool of chapter 1, Two Times Five Equals AOK— that is, calling someone daily for short check-ins—or the fourth tool, sending your Inner Judge on a long cruise.

And remember some of these first aid instruments may fit perfectly into your hand. Others may take a little learning to get used to. And some of them might never work for you. No problem. Like everything in recovery, take what you need. So let's open up this new tool kit and see what's inside.

Tool #1: It Pays to Advertise (Worksheet 3–1)

The billion-dollar industry of advertising is based on a simple premise: people buy what they are familiar with. One perspective for recovery is that you must "market" recovery to your addicted mind. Forces outside of you (beer ads, old drinking and doping buddies, and so on) will be heavily marketing relapse. So you need to launch your own campaign. Marketing studies have shown that it takes seven or more exposures for an advertising message to go from short-term to long-term memory. You want recovery firmly lodged in that long-term memory area of your brain. So you need to begin to bombard it with recovery reminders. Post discreet signs around your work area. It probably is not in your best interest to put a banner in the coffee room saying "Hey, Harvey—remember not to get drunk today!" But you can put up signs that speak only to you. Here are five examples:

- Call first: Call someone outside work and bounce your reactions off them before making a mess!

- Stay curious: Remember, you don't really know what other people are thinking! Don't assume they're judging you.
- Look before you leap...down their throat.
- Now + 5: Take five minutes before overreacting!
- <u>Be</u> a<u>ware</u> of success: Notice what is underlined in this sign—Beware. Recovering people are already wary of misfortune. It is easy to imagine getting fired and going into a bar on your way home to drown your sorrows. However, it is every bit as possible that you could get a promotion and, in your exuberance, drop into that same bar to celebrate. "This one won't hurt. After all, I deserve a reward!" Beware, sudden success can leave you in an upbeat, excited state that can lead to unexpected relapse.

Make up your own signs. Pictures, too. You might choose peaceful scenes that remind you of that place of serenity inside you. Be creative, and surround your workplace with recovery reminders that only you fully understand.

Tool #2: The Craving Deconstructor (Worksheet 3–2)

Cravings don't just happen, and they don't inevitably lead to drinking and drug use. They are like a wave at a ball game. If enough people in one place don't stand up, the wave dies. This is also true of a "crave." It gets started by a trigger, then goes sweeping through you and passes away. Either it becomes a "recovery crave" or a "relapse crave." A recovery crave dies a natural death. A relapse crave ends up with you stoned or drunk or high, and ultimately miserable again.

The Craving Deconstructor takes apart the crave before it becomes a relapse crave. A relapse crave has a four-stage life cycle.

Stage 1: Stimulus. It begins with a trigger. We addressed this problem back in chapter 1. Reduce your exposure to triggers. But when promotions, demotions, arguments, and marriage proposals can be triggers, it should be clear that it is impossible to live in a trigger-free environment. So the Craving Deconstructor isn't designed to take apart the relapse craving at this stage.

Stage 2: Craving. The next stage is the craving itself. Cravings are automatically generated responses of desire. Perhaps saints and yogis can control their desires. But most of us are powerless against the upwelling of physical and emotional hunger coupled with carefully edited memories of how a drink or a joint can make us happy and free from suffering. The goal of recovery (thank God!) is not to control your cravings.

Stage 3: Planning. The third stage in the life cycle of a relapse is the creation of a plan to get a drink, a joint, or a dose.

Stage 4: Action. We then put that plan into effect, in the fourth and final stage, and take action to get high. By the time we get to stage 4 it's too late; the relapse has begun.

Which brings us back to Stage 3, Planning. Before recovery, this was an instantaneous and unconscious stage. We knew exactly what to do and we did it without a moment's reflection. We actually could go into a zombie-like state, and it felt like the car drove itself to the dealer's house.

In recovery, this is where to place the wedge of the Craving Deconstructor and break the relapse craving cycle. The trick is to wake up in the middle of planning how to get loaded. Here are three ways to derail the crave by slowing down the planning phase. They give you time to remember that you are a grateful, recovering, sober person, and not a lush, a stoner, a pill-head, or a junkie.

The Keys to the Kingdom. Put your car keys in a screw-top jar at home or in a zippered case at work. Say a phrase that expresses your feeling of gratitude whenever you open the case or jar to use the keys: "Thank God I am sober today." Or "No more hangovers." Or "I know where I parked the car last night." Or whatever phrase that best expresses your relief at being sober.

When you are headed into automatic pilot, going for the dealer or the bartender, and you unzip the pouch or unscrew the jar to get your keys, all those expressions of gratitude are going to pour forth and interrupt the dazed state. It would be a great time, in that one moment of clarity, to call someone in recovery.

The phone is now your friend. You found out how to use ads in Tool #1. This ad needs to go on top of all your phones, at home, on the cell phone, and at work. It says, "Stay Awake." As you reach for the phone to set up a date with a drinking buddy or call your dealer, look at the sign. Imagine that it automatically heats up whenever you are headed for a relapse, and it will burn your hand if you make that call. But it cools right down when you make recovery calls. So let's do that instead.

Sara had a narrow squeak recently, and her Craving Deconstructor saved the day.

"I placed a CFO in an Internet startup, and made more

money in one week than I had in the previous year. I was flying. I just wanted to let it all rip with celebration. And I wanted some drugs to party with. Insane, I know! But then, I still am plenty nuts. I reached for my little blue book of names, to track down someone who could find me a connection. I have a rotten head for telephone numbers, but a great little book of contacts. Years ago I put a very thick rubber band around my book, on which was written in big bold print, 'One day at a time.'

"As I took off the band I saw the writing, and it was like the spell was broken. All of a sudden I remembered I was in recovery. Then I saw that I was a little crazy. I called my sponsor instead, and celebrated by taking my home meeting out for free coffee after the meeting."

Home, James. One of the trickiest times of the day is coming home after work. Just working hard all day can be a trigger in itself. This is a time of day when cravings raise their wicked heads. Some days we are Hungry, Angry, Lonely, and Tired. And using is just a drive or a stroll away.

It is time for another ad. It says, "Home, James." Put this sign in front of the speedometer of your car if you drive to work or clipped onto your transit pass if you use mass transit. When you see it and move it to drive or to use your ticket, think of the best things you can about home. It may be the quiet or the connection with someone else, the privacy or the friendly chaos. Replace any relapse plan with an image of your home as a refuge. And go straight home. Or better yet, to a meeting.

Tool #3: Drawing the Cloak (Worksheet 3–3)

Work is an ongoing, never-ending series of stressful experiences. Before recovery we might have used "medication" to blunt our sensitivity to all these stimuli. Without that crutch, the impact of a "normal" workday can feel overwhelming.

What we sometimes need is an island of calm, quiet serenity to retreat to in the middle of a chaotic, noisy, harsh day. This tool is designed to give you a mini-vacation, available free anytime and nonaddictive.

The first part of this tool is a cloak. Not an actual cloth one, but one crafted in your imagination. Here are the directions for finding it:

Some evening or weekend when you feel in a peaceful mood and you can be alone for a while, find a comfortable place and read the following visualization. Some folks first read it into a tape recorder and then play it back, so they can listen with their eyes closed. Others just read a sentence, and then close their eyes and imagine what is described. Still others have someone read it to them. Find a way that works for you. Read the visualization, and then take a moment to write down and draw what you saw.

> Settle into a comfortable position. Good. Now just pay attention to your breathing. Feel your chest rising and falling as the air comes in and out. If you notice your mind wanting to grab your attention away from your breath, just sigh, and ask your brain to leave you alone for a little while, and return your focus to your breath. In and out. Gentle. Good. Feel yourself settling down into your breath, and relaxing a little more each time you exhale.
>
> Now imagine that there is a movie screen inside

your mind, which right now is gray, as you breathe in and out. Gradually the screen begins to light up, and you see an image of a place in your life when you were very peaceful, quiet, and content. See the picture of what was around you, and hear the sounds, smell the smells, feel yourself back in that comfortable, calm, serene place. You are there in the movie, just relaxing and enjoying the tranquil mood.

In front of you is an old chest. Look closely at it. It is locked with an ancient iron lock, but you notice that you have the key in your pocket. You open the lock, and then you open the chest.

You find several objects inside. They might be jewels or tools. Pick each one up and examine it. You may be surprised at what you find. If you see nothing, just make something up. All these gifts are yours. Each one will support your recovery. Spend some time getting to know each object.

Finally, in the bottom of the chest there is a cloak. Pull it out and hold it up to look at it. It is beautiful. Take a moment to enjoy how it looks. Now wrap it around your shoulders. It fits you perfectly. As you feel the weight and texture of it, you discover that it is a magic cloak. It has absorbed the stillness, restfulness, and serenity of this place. You know that, whenever you wrap it around you, you will be back in this place, and you will feel the gentleness of this moment.

Each of these gifts is magical. Find a place inside you where you can store each one for the time when you need it. Then close the chest, and again become aware of your breath. As you breathe in and out, the movie screen begins to fade back into gray. You are aware of your body. You feel comfortable and rested.

You remember the gifts you brought back with you, and you understand how they can support your recovery. You open your eyes.

Take some time to write down your experience. If you have some crayons or colored pens, draw your cloak. You will discover for yourself how to use the other gifts you brought back with you. Here is a suggestion for using the cloak to relieve the pressure in your world.

Imagine that it's a particularly stressful day. All the things you start out to do unravel. Everyone is complaining about you. Work sucks. You need a break!

Walk outside or go the rest room, back stairs, or storage closet, or somewhere where you can be alone. Remember your cloak, and wrap it around you. Feel the weight and the texture of it. Sense the tranquillity and peacefulness that glows around you as you sit or stand, protected in your cloak's magic energy. Breathe in the calmness and the quiet. Feel your inner core begin to settle and relax. Stay there a little longer than you think you should, just enjoying the moment and getting more and more grounded. Then wrap your cloak up and put it in its safe place inside you and return to work knowing that your serenity comes from inside you and can't be disturbed by other people's stress.

Tool #4: Gold Stamps
(Worksheet 3–4)

Back in the sixties there was a psychological concept going around called Brown Stamps. The idea went something like this: Remember when there were green stamps? They worked like this; you would go to the store, and along with your groceries, the checkout clerk would give you so many sheets of stamps, depending on how much you spent. You would go home and stick them into redemption books, and when you had enough you could turn them in at the redemption center for real neat things like porch furniture or electric blenders.

Well, psychologists latched onto this idea and said that there are Brown Stamps that folks go around collecting, also. You get a stamp every time you stuff a feeling, every time you act codependently, every time you use a drug to bury your emotions, every time you sell yourself out because of fear. There are lots of ways to collect Brown Stamps! You then get to go home and stick them in your redemption book. When you get enough you can cash them in on some really swell prizes. One book for a weekend binge or a huge righteously angry blowout scene. Two books for an affair. Three for an ulcer. Four for a nervous breakdown. And the grand prize, homicide or suicide.

In your toolbox is another kind of stamp. Gold Stamps are collected every time you support your recovery. I recommend you make a little book you can carry around, and get some stickers, and actually put a stamp in your book every time you strike a blow for your sobriety. You collect stamps for going to meetings, for using recovery tools, like your cloak, or getting the recovery flu. You get a stamp when you successfully make it through a rough bout of craving, or when you have a really tough day and you don't think of using once. Make up your own rules.

Every time you get five stamps in your book you must give yourself something luxurious. Limit the cost to under forty dollars per gift or experience. But do it! A massage, a hot tub, a fine lunch, a beautiful walk, a new pair of cool socks, a book, a scarf, a toy. Some prizes may cost nothing. But reward yourself. You deserve it!

Tool #5: The Denial Destroyer (Worksheet 3–5)

This is "two, two, two tools in one." You will need at least two three-by-five-inch cards.

The handle of the Denial Destroyer is called the BS Detector—it's truth-telling time. On the first card write down all the lies your Inner Addict tells you about drinking and using.

When Sara did this exercise, here was some of the stuff she told me that she wrote on her card. "I need this to sleep. It will get me in the mood to party and have a good time. Sobriety is way too boring. Everybody is doing it. I used to have fun, now all I do is go to meetings. I can't cope without a hit. Just this one time; it's an emergency!" You know the lines. Write small and fill up both sides of the card with them.

Now take this card, and read each lie out loud. After you read each one say the ritual phrase, "No, that is a lie!" If you don't fully believe that the statement is a lie, keep repeating, "No, that is a lie!" even though you are arguing with yourself. After a while you may let yourself see the truth. If you can't get past one, start making some phone calls to your support people, and talk with them about it. You must know, with no doubts, that this is a lie, or your Inner Addict will slam you over the head with it. Stay with that statement until you know the statement is a trick and is false. Only when you can say with vehemence, "No, that is a lie!" can you go on to the next one.

When you have finished all the statements, set fire to the card and burn it up entirely. No more lies. From now on when the Inner Addict tries to talk you into breaking your sobriety by telling you one of these lies, you will simply say, "No, that is a lie."

If the BS Detector is the handle, the blade of the Denial Destroyer is called the Truth Record. To make this tool, pick up the other card. On one side write down a list of the trials, struggles, and messes that resulted from your drinking or drug taking. You don't have to write out a whole AA Fourth Step, only the highlights (or lowlights) of the worst moments. Use just a few words so that you remember.

The first time she did this, Sara's card read, "The DWI in Utah. Not knowing the name of the person in bed next to me the next morning. Breaking my arm. The mess on the rug in my parent's bathroom. Date-raped in Trenton. Hangovers!!! What happened the weekend of July 16th?"

On the other side of the card, list the best of the good things that have come to you since recovery. Sara wrote, "AA. Tight with the band and crew. Mary. Waking up without a hammerhead. Pride. Talking with both my mom and my dad and not ending up yelling at each other. Sue, my sponsee!!! Hope."

This card is a record of the truth about your sobriety and about what came before. Always carry it with you. Add to it when you need to. Anytime you begin to feel that using might be a swell idea, just pull it out and read both sides. The truth shall set you free.

Managing Anger:
The Four C's

Victoria's Story

 Victoria is a professional tennis player, tennis instructor, and co-owner of a prosperous racquet club. She had a "grand slam" anger problem. It was bad during her drinking, but became worse when she could not "medicate" it.

After three months in recovery, she began to feel the only way she could keep her relationships, her tennis students, and her business partner was to return to dosing herself with alcohol. In this chapter, we will explore how you, like Victoria, can use the four C's to find a place of emotional stability.

"For me," Victoria explains, "C stood for Cages. The cages saved me. Batting cages, that is.

"Early in recovery, I often found myself in the middle of frustrating interactions with my business partner. Now understand, we had been fighting for years. It was how we did business together. But before recovery, I used alcohol as medication to calm me down. And sometimes I used being drunk as an excuse to blow up at her. But I didn't know a sober way of handling the anger when it came up. I tried stuffing it all, but I was building up quite a head of steam.

"I really wanted to forcefully demonstrate why she was full of it. Of course, I was completely in the right. I did the only thing I could think of. I would stomp away from the courts and head right for the batting cages. I wanted to go to the bars, but the cages were always a little closer. I don't know squat about baseball, and I don't want to know much more than that. But I would put the machine on slow pitch and mentally paint her face on every ball and blast away. After half an hour or so, I settled down enough to entertain the idea that I might not be 100 percent blameless in the situation."

What is anger? We all know how anger feels: the heat of it, the tenseness of it, and the way it flows through our bodies insisting we do something. Sometimes anger is a burning sensation, so hot and strong we can barely be still. Sometimes it is icy, a hatred that turns our eyes into slits and our thoughts toward resentment and vengeance. Either way it is intense and unmistakable.

The physiologists tell us what they think anger is. For them it is caused by a flood of self-manufactured chemicals pouring into our bloodstream. These chemicals speed up our heartbeat, send blood rushing into our muscles, and shut down our digestion. That tight stomach wasn't just your imagination.

This series of reactions is called the fight-or-flight syndrome and was created to get us ready to attack or to run away. This strategy of supercharging our body has been one of our survival mechanisms since we were living in trees.

The physiologists and evolutionary theorists have made some contributions to our understanding of anger. But their thoughts, while interesting, don't really help too much in managing anger. Let's turn to psychology. One psychological explanation of the cause of anger is that anger is an emotional reaction that comes from unmet expectations. We expect people to be fair, kind, nurturing, polite, considerate, and supportive.

Sometimes they are not. Sometimes people are self-centered (instead of being us-centered), cruel, depriving, rude, inconsiderate, and downright mean. And at other times they are just being themselves, but we see them as monsters (remember that problem with projection that was discussed in chapter 1). The problem is that we expected something from them that they were either unwilling or unable to give us. One possible reaction to this disappointment is anger.

This psychological explanation may help us see why we got angry in the past. We may be able to examine the specific unmet expectation that triggered our reaction. Usually it is too late by then. We have already reacted all over the people who upset us, by blowing up or by icing them.

Next we'll look at anger from a developmental perspective. To understand anger from this perspective we need to understand the foundations of our emotional experiences. Emotions are first experienced in infancy. Over time we get more and more words to define the subtleties of these experiences. We learn to differentiate.

What we call anger or love or resignation or any adult emotion is actually composed of two elements. On the surface we have all the beliefs, definitions, values, history, and words to define and express what we feel.

Underneath that, what actually fuels these experiences are primitive root emotions. There are five primary emotional "colors" of the young child. These are the fundamental pigments out of which, as adults, we paint a rich feeling life. These emotions seem to be "hardwired" into the human psyche:

- *Glad:* Happy, joyous, enthusiastically loving, open, and free
- *Sad:* Depressed, low, melancholic, softly crying, slow, down, and teary
- *Bad:* Ashamed, guilty, self-conscious, self-judging, feeling deficient, and feeling inferior
- *Mad:* Angry, hostile, resentful, hating, loudly crying, vengeful, and aggressive
- *Full:* Contented, peaceful, quietly loving, and satisfied

Each one of these emotions can bring aliveness into our daily experience. That may be obvious when you think of "full" or "glad." But there is aliveness in "sad." It is the rich grief that comes with a real loss that needs to be felt in our hearts. There is also aliveness in "bad." It may express itself as a sincere regret we feel when we hurt another, which leads us to atone for our inconsiderate behavior. And there is certainly a flush of "mad" aliveness when we stand up against injustice.

Each of these emotions also has a dark side and can jeopardize your recovery. "Full" can become complacence, which easily turns into denial. Soon the idea of a few recreational drinks or joints sounds eminently reasonable. "Glad" can become manic. Too often I have heard the tale of a client getting a big promotion and falling off the wagon to celebrate. "Sad" can become hopelessness that makes recovery feel empty and hopeless. And "bad" can turn into wretched self-hatred.

As for "mad," it can instantly turn into resentment, which, according to the Big Book of Alcoholics Anonymous, "destroys more alcoholics than anything else."

"Mad" is a basic part of our programming. We are not going to be able to eliminate it, no matter how hard we try. We need it for strength at times. And besides, we are not "holy" enough to eradicate it from our consciousness.

There is a story about a novice in a monastery who was devoted to the one monk in the order who was never angry. No matter what this wise man faced, he was compassionate, loving, and unruffled. One day the novice was on his hands and knees cleaning a far corner of the kitchen floor. His favorite monk came in and started preparing some food. A stray dog came into the kitchen. The monk first looked around to see if anyone was watching. Not noticing the novice, and thinking himself alone, the monk kicked the mutt in the side to drive him out.

No one escapes anger. The issue is how to manage it skillfully. In the moment of an angry confrontation, you will believe with every cell of your body that you *must* fight for your position. This will make many messes.

The following four C's represent skillful ways of managing anger. This is a four-step program for making sure that anger doesn't disrupt your recovery or your life at work. You will find some of these steps fairly easy and others very hard. The steps are meant to be taken in about the order they are presented here. If you find yourself avoiding one, that may be the very step you need to take to get on the other side of your anger management problem.

Being a recovering alcoholic and living a sober life puts you far ahead of the rest of the pack in managing your anger skillfully. The greatest problem most people face with anger difficulties is acknowledging that they even have such a problem. In recovery, we are already forced to look at all our personal issues that led us to addiction. Often we find that anger plays a role in these problems. You have done your homework already. So what do you do when your emotional temperature is rising?

The Four C's

Chill (Worksheet 4–1)

Absolutely no progress can be made with an anger problem if you do not first take this step. Once you "come to believe" that your anger is having a detrimental effect on your life, you need to stop exploding, in the same way you need to stop drinking or using drugs. Which doesn't mean that you stop feeling the anger. For many that is an impossibility. But it means that you stop letting it out.

You cannot change the direction of a bullet once it has left the gun. In the same way you cannot manage anger once you have sprayed it all over the room. The time for skill comes *before* the explosion, not after.

So use the tool in chapter 1 called S.T.O.P. Stop talking and get away from the confrontation as fast as you can. That gives you the space and time to use the other steps.

Useful phrases to employ in these circumstances are:

- "Can I get back to you about that?"
- "I can see that you're upset, and I'll think about what you said."
- "This isn't a good time to talk; let's do lunch!" (a southern California approach)
- "I want to respond, but I can't right now."
- "I have to go, I can't talk right now."
- "The boss wants to see me; we'll have to talk later."

Are you getting the point here? It is about remembering four things:

1. Nothing is more important than your recovery.
2. Blowing up at people jeopardizes your recovery and your job.
3. You are not going to let anyone else's agenda get in the way of #1 and #2.

4. Don't kid yourself, this is absolutely a matter of life and death. Your recovery may very well hinge on whether or not you get away from that other person without blowing up.

So move away from that person who, inadvertently or deliberately, is about to inspire you to boil over. Get out of there, as politely as you can, and as quickly as you can. In the heat of the conflict, you will not be able to win the argument, prove the other person wrong, and get him or her to apologize to you. Aim instead for emotional survival.

Remember that if you do blow up, *it is not the other person's fault.* No one can make you drink, and no one can make you erupt. You exploded because you did not get out of that situation soon enough. It is almost impossible to hang out with someone who is pissing you off for too long without erupting. So move it! Remember, only you can prevent forest fires.

Channel (See Worksheet 4–2)

Congratulations, you got away mostly unscathed. Now, you're still very churned up inside. It's time for Channeling.

Anger demands action. Anger is definitely a physiological event. Unless you address the physiological component, the body can sabotage all your good intentions. Through understanding the physiology of anger, you can take appropriate measures to discharge the anger energy in a skillful way.

Victoria had a great plan for surfing the flood of hormones that came with her anger. Instead of heading for the bar to try to drown them, she walked into the batting cage, stepped up to the plate, and smacked them out of her system.

Anger demands some sort of physical discharge. This needs to happen *away from* the person you're mad at. In your drinking and drugging days, yelling at people, threatening them, slamming doors, and breaking things were all exciting releases of energy. But they do not work in recovery, because you end up feeling ashamed of yourself or brooding because you were violent toward someone else.

 ### Tool #1: Anger Channels

To honor your body's need for tension release, find some physical release activity. As soon as you can extricate yourself from the situation, go somewhere to release the pent-up energy. Here are some activities that fit the bill:

- Tear up old phone books.
- Smash glass into the recycling containers.
- Roll up the windows of your car and scream.
- Hit the bed with a small baseball bat.
- Throw rocks against a wall.
- Work out vigorously.
- Take it out on a punching bag.
- Rip up old rags.
- Run or walk very hard.
- Climb the stairs in your building as fast as you can.

This tool is a difficult one to use while you are working. Your co-workers and supervisors may not understand why you are ripping up phone books in the middle of the day. Sometimes you must wait until a break to do your release work. But remember that the sooner you get the release, the sooner you will be able to return to center. You can always act as if you have an important appointment somewhere and do some intense stair climbing or power walking.

Being a little sweaty may concern you in terms of keeping your image intact. So what? You're trying to save your life here. No one really cares why you may be a little out of breath. But if you give yourself excuses to skip over this step, eventually you will detonate, and people will really notice that.

If you are an explosive type of person, these kinds of physical activities will feel pretty good. This will be an easier step for you than the Chill step was. But there is another type of person who has anger management problems, the imploded type. For you anger is experienced as a cold hardening. You don't have the problem of yelling at people. You get revenge in subtler ways. You may be the one who gets the explosive types to make fools of themselves. You may have been accused of being critical, judgmental, and fault-finding. This is also an anger problem.

You may find no problem in chilling out, because you have a whole deep freeze filled with stored resentments. The difficulty for you will be in thawing this icy indignation. For you, the physical expression of your anger is a necessity. Until your anger gets a chance to be expelled through your muscles, it will fester inside and contaminate your relationships at work.

So when you get wounded and you feel that icy, vengeful, judgmental energy inside chilling your bones, get away from the situation and start to move your body. Heat up that anger, so it can be released.

Clear

Channeling cleared the physical body; now we need to find release for the emotional part of you. Clearing means using a friend, a sponsor, a therapist, or a coach to vent all the feelings about the situation that well up inside. This usually takes less than four minutes. Once you are finished, you can begin to see the circumstances without all the red highlights.

Tool #2: Cleaning the Slate (Worksheet 4–3)

Here is what you need in order to clear effectively:

- a trained receiver
- four to five minutes in a place where you can raise your voice and say everything you need to say
- a willingness to move beyond cleaning the slate once you are through

You will need to train the person you are going to use to help you get clear. A sponsor, a friend, your therapist, ministers, or counselors are all good folks to recruit for this job. It pays to have a few people in your "cleaning the slate" support network. Some people to avoid using in your network might include your parents, your boss, your intimate partner, your co-workers, and your kids.

This is a technique you can use with either a trained professional or with a friend. I recommend that you train yourself in how to be a "receiver" and trade off supporting and being supported with other recovering folks.

People in your support network need to agree to the following instructions:

Cleaning the Slate is a way of discharging emotional energy, so that it doesn't come back to bite you and those close to you later on. It requires two players: the Clearer and the Receiver.

The first job of the Clearer is to spend not more than five minutes letting out all of his or her feelings about a specific incident. This is not a time to hold back, to be fair, to see both sides of the situation, or to be polite. This is venting time! Spill out all the resentment, frustration, annoyance, and indignation about what happened to you.

The Receiver has three jobs. The first is to encourage the blurting out of all the junk that needs to be released. The second is to keep time. The third is to help the Clearer move to the next stage.

The Receiver needs to match the Clearer's tone and energy, getting right into their high energy. The following are helpful comments to make:

- "Yeah!"
- "That's right!"
- "That sounds horrible!"
- "Tell me some more about that."
- "Bummer!"
- "That must have made you mad!"
- "What else is in there?"

There are two traps a Receiver must avoid. The first is joining the Clearer in judging the other person. It will not help your Clearer to jump on their bandwagon and say, "Oh yeah, that battle-ax, I hate her, too. Did I ever tell you about the time…?" Keep your focus on helping the Clearer say all that he or she needs to say. You don't have to agree or disagree with the content.

The second trap is judging the Clearer. You must not invalidate the feelings that the Clearer is having. You are not being asked to judge. All you must do is help the Clearer open the valve so that feelings can pour forth.

Cleaning the slate is different from blaming, whining, or complaining. Those compelling activities can go on for hours. Cleaning the Slate must not exceed five minutes. It is short and intense. If your Clearer is done in two or three minutes, that's fine. At four minutes give your

Clearer a one-minute warning. Close it off crisply at five minutes. You are responsible for keeping this important boundary.

The final thing the Receiver needs to do is to ask the Clearer what he or she intends to do next about the situation. Just ask that question. Do not advise, comment on the plan, or tell the Clearer the right thing to do. Then wish him or her well.

If the Clearer is not willing to stop after five minutes, you may allow another minute, and then say something like, "I know you could go on for hours. And it feels to me like you have vented some anger about the situation. So, now what do you want to do about it?"

The following is a transcript of a Cleaning the Slate session that Victoria had with her recovery coach. A recovery coach is a specialist in supporting people in later stages of their recovery.

Vic: Boy, this session couldn't have come at a better time! A half an hour ago, I almost went at it again with Sue [her business partner]. I just got back from the batting cages a few minutes before our session. I am pissed!

Coach: Sounds like you need to clear. Let's spend the next five minutes getting you clear. Tell me about being pissed.

Vic: Who does she think she is? We settled this whole issue about expanding to another site last week. I told her it was impossible for me to handle the work I have now, and there was no way I could handle two clubs.

Coach: And that made you mad!

Vic: It sure did. It's like she didn't even hear me. I thought she cared about me. I thought we were in this together. I mistakenly thought she was supporting my recovery. Now the truth comes out. All she cares about is making bucks!

Coach: That sucks, huh?

Vic: If she really cared about me she would know how frag-ile I am right now. I am a mess, and all she cares about is her IRA and her car payment!

Coach: Yeah, don't stop. What else is in there?

Vic: I'm really hurt that she won't listen to me. Yeah, sure she listens great when she agrees with me. But when I put out what I need and it doesn't happen to agree with her long-range plan, she conveniently forgets what I need and keeps hammering away at what she wants.

Coach: Keep going!

Vic: What do I have to do to get her to see my point, smash her over the head with it? I am perfectly willing to do that if that's what it takes. I'll restring the racket myself! (She laughs.)

Coach: Are you through, or is there something more in there that needs to get out?

Vic: Yeah, one more thing. When she needed support with her operation I was there for her 100 percent. I took care of her dog, I visited her as often as the hospital would let me, I ran the whole club myself, and even...

Coach: I just want you to know that we have just another minute to go for this slate-cleaning session. You were say-ing you ran the club and what else?

Vic: I even cleaned her damn BMW. And I was glad to do all that. Because we were in this together. Now when she has to make a few sacrifices, where is she?

Coach: You're disappointed.

Vic: Yeah, I am. But I can feel myself running down a little. After all, she did pitch in when I went to treatment.

Coach: So, Victoria, have you cleared all the anger about the conversation with Sue?

Vic: Yeah, I guess so.

Coach: So, what is next with Sue?

Vic: I guess I'll use the Ladder with her.

Conflict Management

Handling the conflict without exploding in anger is a topic worthy of an entire book itself. One way to work with highly charged situations is to use a coaching tool called the Ladder. By using a predetermined set of three magic phrases, you are able to express your experience in a way that is not an attack and that might even open up a fruitful discussion about the topic.

 ### Tool #3: The Ladder (Worksheet 4–4)

Begin by asking if you could talk with the person you have a conflict with for a little while, without him or her interrupting. Let the other person know that when you are finished you have some questions you need to ask, so you can better understand what that person meant.

You begin with the first of three phrases: "I want to share what I heard you say to me." In this way you are owning that you only have your memory to rely upon, and you give the listener an opportunity to remind you of a part that you may have forgotten or glossed over. You then give the factual details as you remind the other person of what he or she said to you.

The second phrase to use is this: "And here is the story I made up about it." Then you briefly share how you understood what you heard. Here is your interpretation, but it is presented as a story in your head, rather than as the absolute truth that you want to ram down the other's throat.

Finally you say, "I want to check out what was really going on with you." The only cure for conflict is listening, and that must begin with you.

Here is how Victoria used the Ladder when she got together with Sue: "Sue, when we talked this morning, I heard you ask about expanding our facility. I made up a story that you purposely ignored our talk the other night when I told you I was too shaky to handle that much more responsibility. I'm checking out to see what was really going on with you."

The Ladder is not a foolproof way of getting through conflict. And you may have to back away from this interaction if you start getting too defensive and explosive, or if you feel the other person is just out to make you suffer. Back away without exploding, and return to the chill step. Try again when you have better control.

The attempt to resolve the conflict might leave you with some unfinished business. Unfinished business can breed resentment. "What about paying them back for how they have used and abused me?" you may mutter. The issue of vengeance is central in working with anger. Here is a little exercise that will help you gain clarity on this issue.

Tool #4: Vengeance Exercise (Worksheet 4–5)

Answer the first two items before reading further.

1. List ten times when you really blew up.
2. List five times when you held your temper in and didn't attack the other person.

Here are examples from Victoria's lists: For Item 1 she wrote, "I finally laid into my ex-lover about how I felt hurt and abused." For Item 2 she wrote, "I didn't go after Sue when she talked about opening another racquet club." Before reading on, stop to write your two lists.

Now, next to each item on your lists, write down what the long-term results of your actions were. For example, the result that Victoria wrote for her first item was "My ex-lover and I haven't talked since I blew up at him." After the second item she wrote, "Sue and I ended up having a decent conversation about what we both needed for the rest of this year."

After writing your results, look at your lists and ask yourself who gets hurt in the long run when you vent and try to pay the other person back. Use this list to ask yourself if vengeance is worth the momentary pleasure and release that it brings.

Some conflicts don't get resolved. Some stories have miserable endings. Some people just want to hurt you. And there are some people whom you keep hurting. Sometimes all you can do is walk off the battlefield and dissolve the relationship, or get transferred, or avoid the other person like an Ebola virus. That's life.

But Victoria and Sue just opened their fourth racquet club. They are still arguing, but doing it much more skillfully.

CHAPTER FIVE

Out of Work

Remember that stress test you took back in chapter 1? You would score 47 points just by getting fired. And that doesn't even take into account the stresses placed on your relationships with partner, or spouse and family. Losing your job is one of the most devastating and misunderstood of the traumas that happen in adult life. This chapter has some tools and perspectives for weathering it intact.

In Western countries our jobs are a large part of the answer to the question, "Who am I?" This was not always true. In ancient Greece, your class and your city-state established your identity. In medieval Europe, you knew who you were based on your kingdom and your class. In colonial America, you were your family, your creed, your trade, and your colony.

Today we move an average of every three years. The U.S. divorce rate has tripled in the past thirty years, and today more than half of all marriages end in divorce. The upper class and the lower class are moving further and further apart, and most people are being homogenized into the middle class. Who are we?

In modern American culture, you are what you do. Almost every introduction begins with your name and what you do for a living. Our job lies at the core of who we take ourselves to be.

When you lose your job, be it through downsizing, early retirement, firing, or by choice, you also lose a part of yourself. It is like a physical part of you, an arm or a leg, is missing.

Most of us need both extrinsic (outside ourselves) and intrinsic (within ourselves) acknowledgment. Some monks, night watchpersons, and fire spotters posted on towers in forests far away from any town seem content being solitary. The rest of us need the touch, connection, and appreciation of others in order to feel at peace.

Much of that positive affirmation comes from work. Some recent studies of Western family life find that one reason both women and men are spending less time with their families is that they get more rewards at work than they do at home. Family is dropping in the list of things we use to build our sense of identity, and work is rising. In these studies, people report that at work they get seen and appreciated for what they contribute. At home they face an unending stream of demands for more— more time, more money, more effort—and get very little appreciation.

When your job gets pulled away it leaves a great vacuum in your life. If we are what we do and we are barred from doing it, we start to lose a sense of who we are. Depression, confusion, resentment, and loss take up residence in our minds, and they don't seem in any hurry to depart.

When you choose to leave a job, you usually adjust more easily. When you are fired or unexpectedly forced out, however, you can go into a grief process every bit as profound as if a close friend had died. This pain and stress can powerfully affect your recovery.

Expected Termination

It's hard to be fired from a job you hate or a job you knew you were about to quit anyway. Of course there is some relief. The other shoe finally landed. And the resentment you already have toward your supervisors and your work feels like a buttress, a support for you. "See, I always knew they were rotten! This just proves it."

Even so, getting fired hurts. Downsizing, early forced retirement, or layoff—it really doesn't matter. You end up feeling rejected and lousy about yourself. That Inner Judge we talked about in chapter 1 has all kinds of new material to use to attack and condemn you.

Healing this trauma usually requires three things: time (three to six months before the shame and anger fade), a new job, and some work on your Inner Judge. The tool in the first chapter about sending your Inner Judge on vacation will help turn down the volume on the negative self-talk.

Unexpected Termination

When you get unexpectedly fired, the situation is much more difficult to manage, as Harry describes so well:

Harry's Story

Harry came into therapy two months into his dark days after getting fired. Much of my work with him was grief work, listening to his painful story again and again, accepting him without needing him to get it all together, and hanging out with him as his depression slowly lifted.

"I had it made. I was six months clean and sober. I had a job that paid good money. I was an assistant plant

manager, and had my eyes focused on a management position up at corporate headquarters.

"One day, in what I thought was a pretty polite manner, I let a headquarters guy who was second-guessing one
of my decisions know that I had everything under control,
and that he didn't have to worry about it. OK, maybe my
voice was a little testy, but I was still courteous.

"A month later the plant manager told me I had three
hours to pack up my desk and move out. It came totally
out of the blue. She felt bad, I could tell. She gave me some
lame-o excuse about productivity and downsizing, and I
knew she was lying. I knew where the order came from,
and there wasn't a damn thing I could do about it.

"I kept coming up with revenge plans to get back at that
SOB in corporate who was responsible for me getting fired.
I kept reciting passionate speeches to the chairman of the
board denouncing management. I couldn't face my former
co-workers, and I couldn't stop obsessing, resenting, and
missing my old job. I kept worrying that I would never be
able to hold down a good job again. I worried that I would
never have enough energy and self-confidence to even
look for a decent job again."

When you're fired you feel powerless, angry, hurt, and
resentful: a relapse minefield. In the treatment of post-
traumatic stress disorder, one of the best forms of help is
repeated storytelling. So, too, in getting fired. Healing your
pain after being fired requires finding venues for telling
the story of your firing again and again. Each time you tell
it, you discharge a little more of the energy that binds you.
Use the Cleaning the Slate tool a lot in this process (Worksheet 4–3).

Living Jobless

The good news about not having a job is that it gives you lots of time to devote to your recovery. That sounds like a sick joke, but actually it is a good piece of advice. Sometimes that's the best you can do.

This is how it was for Harry:

"It wasn't fair, but I wasn't going to drink over it. I started going to a meeting a day, and working the program pretty hard. I figured that I would be back on my feet and in another job within a month.

"Yeah, right! The next six months were horrible. I couldn't get a good night's sleep. I was moody and irritable. I ached, and generally felt lousy. Feeling as bad as I was, how was I supposed to make a great impression at a job interview? I took a low-paying menial job, just because I was too depressed to do anything else and I had to eat. I stopped looking in the Sunday classifieds. My world kind of collapsed to driving a forklift during the day, going to a meeting in the evening, and staying up late staring at the TV.

"Nine months after I was fired, I resurfaced. The dark cloud passed, and I could start feeling my old self again. But that nine-month coma was the hardest time so far in my recovery.

"I quit my crummy job and hit the want ads again, and within a month was working at the job I am in now, and I am a lot happier. I can see how that job I thought I loved really had me in a box. They were never going to let me get into management. I was dreaming. Today, I am a vice president of my company."

For a while after being fired you will be living with "occupational bereavement disorder" (a term I just coined). Some of the symptoms are listed here:

- sleep disturbance
- irritability and outbursts of anger
- difficulty concentrating
- recurrent fantasies of revenge
- poor appetite or overeating, or both
- depression and anxiety

You may be in for a season of depression, repeated ill-
nesses, fatigue, anxiety, and frustration. You need to find
ways of accepting that you're only operating on one cylin-
der and that this condition may be with you for a few
months.

Go to ninety meetings in ninety days, not because you
are in danger of slipping, but because you need the love,
support, and structure that the program gives us. Use all
the tools you got in chapters 1 and 3, and be gentle with
yourself.

Don't let the Inner Judge get on your case. Instead come
back to the truth: you are clean, sober, growing, working
your program, and staying awake. That is a miracle that
you helped create. No layoff, no loss of any kind can take
that from you. Only that Judge/Addict team inside your
head says otherwise. Tell them both to get lost, and make
a support call.

You need all the support you can get, just like a newcomer. Even though we have some recovery under our
belt, we still get to use that support when we need to. On
really hard weeks, go back to basics, and use all the tools
in the checklist in exercise 1–5 (in appendix 3). If things
are going sideways at home, think about having several
couple or family sessions with a counselor. Let the counselor know your financial situation, and ask what can be
done in one or two sessions. You will be surprised how an
impartial third party, skilled in communication, can help.

Even though money may be tight, it is still important for everybody close to you to learn how to interact skillfully under this high level of stress.

Looking for Work

The Chinese character for crisis is formed from the character for "danger" combined with the character for "opportunity." Katherine taught me what this feels like from the inside, as she healed from an explosive firing.

Katherine's Story

"The odds of me staying straight were less than zero. One, I was a strung-out teenage hooker. Two, I was black. Three, I was pregnant. No hope, right? Well, I beat all the odds, but just barely.

"So many of my sisters who were working with me chased after the pipe and let their kids get taken away from them. I really wanted to, but my mother's and my grandmother's voices in my head kept telling me that nothing was more important than my baby. So I got on the Greyhound and went back home.

"Kicking rock, pregnant, was a total bitch. My momma was great, just hugged me and asked no questions. My family's pastor and his wife came out of the woodwork and showed up in a huge way, letting me talk with them for hours when I really wanted to go back to the streets. I could tell them all the stuff about what happened to me and about wanting to base, stuff I couldn't tell anyone else. They just cared and never judged me. I still don't know what they saw in this wasted, ragged, eighteen-year-old loser, but they believed in me, and prayed for me, and gave me the spirit to stay clean.

"I started going to NA. I worked the Steps. I had my baby straight, and breast-fed her drug-free milk. Thanks to my church, I got a job for a year and a half working part-time at a convenience store.

"Bad things happen to good people. The married store manager, who I really trusted, put a hard move on me, and I told him what I thought of that. Right there, BAM! I was out of work.

"I wanted to call it quits. I was never going to amount to anything. Who did I think I was, anyway? I wanted to leave my little girl at Momma's and split. I wanted to get back on that bus. I wanted some crack so bad. Instead, I walked down to my church, and sat alone for two hours, praying and crying. Then I went to Momma's and lay for a long time hugging my baby.

"I was kind of crazy for a long while. I didn't drink or dope, but I felt real sorry for myself. I kept seeing that man's pimply face, leering at me. I got a couple of temp jobs, but I kept expecting to get screwed, and, with my attitude, I ended up screwing myself.

"So, one day I was playing with Melika in the park, out of work again. And this big peace came upon me. It was like something from the Bible. I was calmer than I had ever been before. I saw my whole life. I saw how the love, and the freebase, and the friends, and the pimps, and johns, and the pastor, and Momma, and the sleazy store manager all wove together to bring me to this park, and to my beautiful daughter. And it was all as it should be.

"I knew in that moment that I had nothing to fear. I could make it, and God would show me how. I also was real clear about what is important to me, and what isn't. My family, Melika, and my church are important. My history isn't.

"The next day I found out how to take classes in the

local community college. I never paid much attention in class back in high school before I dropped out. Too many guys, too much dope.

"I found out that I was damn smart, and that I was good with computers. I was good with people, too. Who would have known? Today, six years later, I have a full-time job as a computer technician and I have my eyes on a management slot. And I own my own house."

Katherine is building a life firmly based on her values. She has been able to take the blow of being fired and transform it into a gift. But it took almost a year of being in the pain before her clarity came. That is the way it is with trauma—it has its own timetable, and all our pushing only makes it worse.

With both Harry and Katherine there was a transition period, in which they worked their program, had their anger and "attitude," took manageable jobs, and made it through. Then, when the mourning was finished, they both stepped into their power.

In order to live from your power it is important to know what you want and why. A value is a quality we prize in ourselves. I used to think of them as virtues. When I was a Boy Scout we learned, "A scout is trustworthy, honest, loyal, helpful, courteous, kind, obedient, cheerful, thrifty, brave, clean, and reverent." I thought those were values. Unfortunately they usually ended up being unattainable standards.

Value, in the common meaning, is the worth we put on things and experiences. From this perspective we are what we own. Value, the way I am using it, is more about our essential nature than it is about our possessions.

Values are what pull you out of bed each morning. They are the experiences that make life worth living. They give meaning to us when life gives us difficult cards to play.

Values are "who you be" more than "what you do." Some of Katherine's values are her love of her daughter, her faith, and her capacity to create a home.

Life coaching works intensely with values. In my training as a coach at Coaches Training Institute I learned some tools for identifying your deepest values. Using the following tool you can gain clarity on what your values are:

Tool #1: Values Clarification (Worksheet 5–1)

We are going to make a list of your core values. First write out the answers to the following questions:

1. Think of a time when your life was great. The world appreciated what you had to bring it. Paint that time in your mind's eye. Now look at what values were being honored by others at that time. What qualities that you possess were being seen by your world?
2. Now think of a time when you were angry and upset. Pick a time when someone was walking all over you. Which of your values were being disrespected in that moment?
3. What makes you feel like your life is a success? If you notice that there are things (a Rolex, a Saab convertible) that make you feel successful, what do those things say about you? What values emerge when you look here?
4. What would make your life totally fulfilling?
5. What is most important to you?
6. What are some things your friends know about you that you might not even include on a list of values, because they are so apparent to you?

Core values. Now, from your written answers, start pulling out a list of at least ten core values. Other ones may pop up. Include them on your list. This might be quite a long list.

Here is an abridged version of the work Harry did with this tool.

1. Vacationing in Hawaii. Lying on the beach alone with my wife. Not some ritzy resort, but secluded, and beautiful. My love of nature, and need for rest, and love of my wife were being honored.

2. Getting fired. My loyalty to my employer and my willing-ness to work hard were dumped on.

3. The first thing I thought of was owning a red MGTD con-vertible from the fifties. Then I thought of sitting behind the president's desk of my own company. The sports car would show my flair for adventure and that I am unconventional. The president's chair would reflect that I am a hard driver, and a damn good leader.

4. When I can have my own company and take care of my employees, so they love their jobs. And travel whenever and wherever I want to. Maybe raise some kids someday. Then I will feel fulfilled.

5. My wife, doing a good job, enjoying my life; it's the only one I've got.

6. I am intelligent and have a great sense of humor.

From this he built a list of core values:

My Values
- Love
- Being in nature
- Hard work
- Loyalty to my family and my work
- Creativity

- Care about the people I manage
- Being unconventional
- Intelligence
- Humor
- Being a visionary
- Adventure

Prioritize. The next job is to choose the top five values from your list. When you have them, prioritize them and number them, from most central and important to least. This is hard. But which values must you live, no matter what?

Harry's list went:

1. Loyalty
2. Love
3. Hard work
4. Caring
5. Being unconventional

When you are finished, next to each one of these five values, put a number from 1 to 10, scoring how much you manifest this value in your daily life today. A 1 means you think this is a really good idea and sometime soon you need to start honoring it. A 10 means that you honor it with every waking breath you take. (Keep the Inner Judge out of this. There are no wrong answers.)

Harry's rating looked like this:

Loyalty 8
Love 6
Hard work 9
Caring 4
Being unconventional 5

He said about this exercise: "Damn, I am a great employee! I really realized three things. One, I need to spend some more quality time with my wife. Two, I am letting the details of my work get in between me and the folks that I supervise. It's time for some good old-fashioned schmoozing and getting back in connection with them. And finally, I think no one at work knows what a wild and crazy guy I am. My wife sure knows, but I have been presenting myself as pretty straitlaced. I need to bring some fun into work."

Living values. The final step is to make these values come alive for you. So far this is just an intellectual exercise. Now we want to give these words flesh and bones and blood.

Take each of the five values, and, in your imagination, see an image that embodies that word. Don't force it. Start with a color or a shape, or just let your mind wander. When an image comes, write it down next to the value. Keep at it until you feel something click. Then go on to the next one. Some people are image-oriented, and some are word-oriented. If images are not your strong suit, talk about this value with someone who knows you, and together until you find an image that vibrates.

Harry listed as his values:

Loyalty—"Dutch," my dog, the boxer I had as a kid. He helped raise me.

Love—"John Walton." The dad on the old TV show *The Waltons.* A great provider who loved his wife and family.

Hard worker—"The ram." Like from the song, he wouldn't quit: "Oops, there goes a million kilowatt dam."

Caring—"Ghandi." He was rich and entitled, and he gave all that up because he cared so much about the Indian people.

Being unconventional—"Whitewater Guide." I always wanted that job.

Knowing what you stand for is a great support when you are getting ready to go back out in the employment world. I recommend that you have a session or three with a career counselor to clean up your résumé, to strategize how to deal with getting fired, and to find matches between your values and possible occupations. A good career counselor is money well spent. For further work on values I recommend the book *Co-Active Coaching* by Laura Whitworth, Henry House, and Phil Sandahl (Davies-Black Publishing, 1998). Finally, read chapter 10, "Dare to Dream Again," and decide what your work in this lifetime really is. Best of luck!

CHAPTER SIX

Traveling and Entertaining
Clean and Sober

It all began with a business trip.

Bill's Story

"I began to hang around Wall Street again, and, through a chance acquaintance, I had scraped up a brokerage shop. I insulated myself into a proxy row that involved control over a little machine tool company in Akron, Ohio.

"In May of 1935 a party of us went out to Akron fighting for control of the company. I could already see myself as its new president. But when the chips were down, the other side had more proxies and our side got licked. My newfound acquaintances were discouraged, and they left me in Akron's Mayflower Hotel with only about ten dollars in my pocket.

"They departed on Friday. On Saturday, Mother's Day eve, I was pacing up and down the hotel lobby, wondering what I should do. The bar at one end of my beat was filling up rapidly. I could hear the familiar buzz of conversation in there. Down at the other end of the lobby I found myself pausing at a church directory. Then I was seized with a thought: I'm going to get drunk. Or no, maybe I won't get drunk; maybe I'll just go into that bar and drink some ginger ale and make some new acquaintances. Then I panicked. That was really a gift! I had never panicked before at the threat of alcohol. Maybe this meant that my sanity had been restored. I remembered that, in trying to help other people, I had stayed sober myself. For the first time I deeply realized it. I thought, 'You need another alcoholic as much as he needs you!'"

—*Alcoholics Anonymous Comes of Age*
(Alcoholics Anonymous World Services, 1957)

Bill Wilson went to the phone and eventually met up with Dr. Bob, and AA was born. Unfortunately, before this trip there were many other business trips in which Bill ended up drunk and out of control.

In our addicted years, drugs and alcohol seemed such useful tools for business travel and entertaining. We could drink away our anxiety about flying and about being in a strange city. We could take drugs to help us go to sleep, and other drugs to jack us up into high gear when we woke up. We could lubricate social situations that otherwise might make us nervous. We could create cheeriness in our clients that could win them over to our presentation. We could medicate our loneliness by going into any bar and making friends or picking up dates. If our trip was successful we could use drugs and alcohol to celebrate. If we failed they could console us.

Traveling and entertaining without psychoactive chemical crutches is more challenging. Fortunately for all us recovering folks, the social conventions in the world of business have changed toward moderation. The three-martini lunch is a thing of the past in many areas. Refusing a drink is no longer considered a social faux pas. Even admitting to being in recovery is acceptable in some places.

That is the good news. The bad news remains bad. Lunch for many construction crews and assembly line workers is a six-pack and something to be washed down with it. Criminal lawyers still get guys who dump a bag of blow on their desk and say, "Here's your retainer." The drug abuse rate among doctors and nurses is rising. The cost to the consumer in the United States of drug and alcohol abuse is measured in billions of dollars. So the dragon is still loose.

Here are four traveling tools you can pack along with your toothbrush.

Tool #1: A Travel Guide

How do you protect yourself and your recovery? Bill W.'s example still holds. The very best thing you can do when traveling to a strange city is find a local AA or NA meeting. Call the day before you leave. Information will give you the number of an intergroup fellowship office in the area, or see appendix 2 for Web sites that will help you find a meeting or intergroup fellowship office. Ask the folks in the office to recommend a meeting for each night you are there.

Have that information handy, written down in your pocket. Also take two twenty-dollar bills and stuff them in your wallet or purse, way back in a secret compartment. This is your cab fare. You don't need to be a geography expert; just leave the driving to them.

You may choose not to go to a meeting. But if dropping into a bar or breaking open one of those little bottles in that refrigerator in your hotel room or looking for a street dealer begins to appeal to you, call a cab right now, and get to that room of friendly strangers.

Tool #2: Not One!

It's about those little bottles. They are very dangerous. And they are everywhere: in hotel rooms, on trains, in convenience stores—I have seen them even in gas stations! They look so harmless and so cute. How can anything lethal come in such an adorable little play container?

This symbol represents the essential key to a relapse-free recovery: It means, "Not One!" Not one little bottle. Not one hit off that doobie. Not one sip, snort, lick, alcoholized dessert, or line of blow. Not "Just one more time and then I'll be good." Put this sign on that little refrigerator in your hotel room. Put it in your daytimer after 7:00 P.M. Put it anyplace that will help you remember that all you need to do is avoid that first one.

Tool #3: Euphemisms

There are some business situations in which you just don't want to say, "Actually, I don't want a drink (or a joint) because I am a stone addict and I can't handle just one." While it is true, it may not best serve your business interests.

Refusing drugs is usually acceptable behavior. Refusing alcohol can still be momentarily awkward. Here is a list of ways of excusing yourself from addictive behavior:

- "No, thank you anyway."
- "My doctor has recommended I don't drink."
- "I am allergic to alcohol."

- "I have alcohol toxemia."
- "I am not drinking today."
- "Not right now, thanks."

You can add to this list. I used the allergic to alcohol line for a while, until I got more comfortable with just "No, thanks." These days, not so many people inquire after you refuse a drink.

 ### Tool #4: Clean Your Environment

The world is not an alcohol- and drug-free environment. You are continually barraged by messages that tell you that relief, friendship, love, passion, and terminal happiness is a pill or a sip away.

But you can do what you can to remove temptation from your immediate environment. As you board the airplane, you can tell the flight attendants to please refrain from offering you alcoholic beverages. You probably think this is stupid and perhaps a little obnoxious. They usually forget and ask anyway. But what you have done is to eliminate a back door escape for yourself. Burn those bridges! By admitting you are in recovery you will keep yourself from blowing it with "Just one little beer, because I am afraid of flying." And when the plane is circling Dallas and the booze really starts to flow, it won't be flowing into you.

When making hotel reservations, insist that the refrigerator be removed or that all alcoholic beverages be removed from it. This is not an unusual request. The hotel staff may forget, in which case you can remind them when you check in. Few of us are comfortable in a strange city sleeping next to such temptation. You do not have to have willpower of steel. At least in your own private space, you have the right to make it a drug- and alcohol-free environment.

When dining, turn your wineglass upside down or ask the waiter to remove it. "I won't be drinking tonight" will work. That way you cannot accidentally get served wine. At parties, always ask if the punch has alcohol in it or if there is an alcohol-free alternative. (It was embarrassing, but once, not so surreptitiously, I spit the toxic punch back into the glass and poured it into a nearby fern. Poor fern.) There will be sparkling water available at most social gatherings these days.

When you have to entertain, make it an alcohol-drug-free event. You might serve carbonated apple juice, soft drinks, punch, and mineral water. There are a surprising number of nonalcoholic alternatives on the market these days. Some recovering folks drink nonalcoholic champagne, nonalcoholic wine, and near beer. But others worry that it can lead back to drinking. Find your own truth, but be very careful. "Alcohol-free" beer has alcohol in it, and knocking back a six-pack of near beer is not sobriety.

If you must have alcohol at your event, keep it in the beer and wine category and get someone else besides yourself to buy it, serve it, and take home the remains after the event. It is best if you can geographically separate the bar from the place where nonalcoholic drinks are served. This supports everyone in recovery who is attending your event.

Traveling and entertaining can actually be more enjoyable sober. You will find that you show up more present and more genuine. Whenever your path intersects with drugs and alcohol, simply stay as far away from it as you can. When having to deal with any addictive substance, good advice comes from the Bible. Remember "Lead us not into temptation, but deliver us from evil." Sounds like a good plan! Stay away from temptation and you won't need to rely on willpower.

PART TWO

The First Year

A Gradual Awakening

■

CHAPTER SEVEN

Creating Support

We can't do recovery alone. We already tried abstinence alone. Starting out with New Year's resolutions or grim determination, we would embark on a program of "No more!" We would eliminate hard liquor, but an occasional beer was OK. We would swear off all drugs, except for maybe just one hit off a joint at a party. We would be drug- and alcohol-free for a week (or maybe even a month) to convince ourselves that we really didn't have a problem. Eventually we would end up right back in it again.

But when other people are with us in our recovery, we are able to do things we never thought we would be able to do alone. We let others in, and not just the folks sitting around the table in self-help groups, but lots of other people. Gail let in her whole office.

Gail's Story

 Gail was sure that she needed chemical help to do her job. She was the escrow coordinator in a small but busy title company. She was overwhelmed. Eight hours weren't enough to do all her work. Late-night sessions were wearing her down. Coffee soon was replaced by diet pills, and finally by carefully doled-out lines of cocaine, which she called her "little helpers." After long hours at her desk, she went home tense and unable to sleep. Knocking off a few drinks was the only way she could calm herself down enough to pass out and finally sleep.

"I finally faced the fact that I had a problem with the drinking and the drugs. But I was afraid of losing my job. I had to keep churning out the paperwork. I didn't want to go into treatment, for two reasons. One, I needed my chemical crutches. And two, if I was gone, the paperwork would just pile up, waiting for me to return. Without the help of drugs, I'd never be able to log the hours it would take to catch up. I didn't dare tell anyone how weak and desperately obsessed with my 'little helpers' I had become. I was trapped!

"I gave up and went to my boss. He was a real mentor to me, and I knew my addiction was letting him down in a way that felt awful to me. I was ready to be fired. I just couldn't handle the lying anymore.

"He was great. He told me about his brother who had a drug problem and who kept getting treatment and then falling back into using again. He was very firm: I had to go into residential treatment if I wanted to continue to work there. We started brainstorming about how the office could handle the extra work, and I surprised him. I said, 'Look, Drew, I am not going to try to be private about this. My problem has affected everyone here, and I am just going to tell the office that I have a drug and alcohol problem, and I am going into treatment to kick it.'

"I am really glad I chose that road. Most of the people were very surprised. I don't look like your stereotypical drug addict! Because they didn't really believe me, I think some of them were annoyed at having to pick up the extra workload when I was away at treatment. There are only eight people working in our office, and my being gone was rough on all of them. But you know what? They did it. I guess I wasn't so irreplaceable after all.

"They were glad for a lot of reasons to see me come back. Even at 50 percent I could do enough so that they could go back to their already overwhelming workload.

"I decided that I was going to do a part of my Ninth Step early. I wanted to go back to work and make it a real new beginning. I made it a point during the first two weeks back from the hospital to have lunch one-on-one with each of them and tell them my addiction story. They became a part of my recovery support family.

"I encouraged them to share stories of how my 'spaciness' or irritation or agitation when I was using had affected them. At first they didn't share much, but as time went on and they saw what I was like sober, they would tell me how hard it had been to work with me before recovery.

"Some moved a little away from me. I know that at least one of them had her own addiction problems, which she didn't want to face. But four of them, including my boss, got closer to me than I ever expected or imagined. Good thing, too.

"My first five years in recovery were hard. I found out that my husband had been having affairs for years, and I ended up divorcing him. I had a bout with breast cancer. My friends at work were right there for me. Because I had already shared my most shameful secret with them, it was much easier to let them in to support me through the rest of it. Thank God for their caring! It kept me sober and grateful."

Gail showed me how someone could boldly step out of a framework of shame and distrust and enlist the caring support of her co-workers. It wasn't all good news. She shared the resistance and judgment that some of those folks had about her being so public with her need. She heard questions like:

"Did you really need to go into treatment? Why didn't you just quit?"

"Why are you still going to those groups? Aren't you over it by now?"

"Aren't you just trading one addiction for another? First it was drinking, and now it's AA."

"Work isn't really the place to be sharing your personal problems. Why don't you just keep them to yourself?"

Contained within each of these questions is a belief that it is better to handle your problems by yourself. In fact, there is a whole web of beliefs and judgments about independence and dependence. The issue of healthy dependence is so critical to a successful recovery that we need to take a closer look at it.

I needed an objective expert to analyze the rejection of dependence in our culture. Fortunately, I happened to run into an alien, extraterrestrial anthropologist named Zog, who was studying humans in the hive called San Francisco for its doctoral dissertation at the Interplanetary University of Orion. Here is the introduction to that study.

Zog's Research

A vast majority of the species Homo sapiens is made up of worker animals. They spend from eight to fourteen hours a day toiling in groups. Like the other communal primates (baboons and chimpanzees), human work groups arrange themselves in a hierarchical authority structure. Individuals are closely monitored, and there is a very narrow range of approved behaviors. Even clothing is severely restricted, with different work groups allowed different

costumes. Generally the higher up in the authority structure they are placed, the more restrictive, monotone, and
uncomfortable the clothing they are forced to wear.

Most workers are unhappy with their jobs. Most resent
those who belong to groups with more authority than
their group. They also blame their lack of success on those
incompetent workers who belong to groups under them
in the authority structure. Work is generally a very unhappy, serious, and unpleasant experience.

I immediately perceived four behavior patterns, common to all members of this species:

1. This is a fiercely communal species. They live in large
groupings, sometimes numbering in the millions. The historical record indicates that this urban clumping behavior has been the norm for a majority of the population for
at least five thousand years.

2. Individuals are primarily motivated by their need for
contact with others of their species. This contact can be
direct, for example, through touching, talking, making
visual contact, smelling, and tasting each other. If direct
contact is not available, they are satisfied with indirect
contact. They will listen to others' voices, transmitted
through radio waves, or stare for hours at images broad-
cast through their television sets. Often they fall asleep to
these images, and then are awakened in the morning to
the sound of their timed radio receiver turning on, with
voices exhorting them to go into the day.

3. Individuals identify their core nature by their partici-
pation in groups. When asked, "Who are you?" they near-
ly always respond by naming groups they are affiliated
with. They begin with familial or work groups, and then

go on to describe how they serve those groups. They are at a loss to define themselves outside of their connections to others.

They become mentally and physically ill if isolated from others of their species. Infants require extensive touch and stimulation from their rearing commune in order to thrive. Children can be damaged cognitively, emotionally, and even physically if they do not receive this attention.

Adults, when separated from their work groups (they call this being "fired" or "laid off"), become disorganized, depressed, and even violent. A significant majority of male elders die within one year of being permanently exiled ("retired") from their work group.

4. Their strong impulse to clump together has resulted in larger and larger hives. Ten thousand years ago, the hive may have consisted of twenty to thirty individuals in a migrating hunter-gatherer group. Then came villages, towns, city-states, countries, empires, and global alliances. With innovations in technology, they are on the brink of creating a global hive, in which any individual can communicate with any other individual with no concern for geographical or political boundaries.

What I find so fascinating with humans is not the existence of these instincts. Rather, it is the widespread denial of them. No, denial is not a strong enough word. The humans whom I have studied vehemently repudiate their communal instinctual nature. In fact, they despise their own dependence on others.

From soon after birth until death, they devoutly deny their need for each other and strongly identify with their own separateness and autonomy. The psychological structure, and the tension that fuels it, is what I call the "myth of autonomy." It is particularly dominant in the culture that I studied.

Individuals around me were continually barraged with graphic and subliminal messages that promoted these core ideas:

- You and you alone are personally responsible for all the good and bad things that happen to you.
- You are the master of your life. You can do it alone.
- You will be judged by your actions, not by the actions of those around you.
- You are free to choose anything, and the influence of those around you is no excuse. You alone are responsible for what you choose.
- If you express your need for others very often, you are considered immature or mentally ill.

These concepts may be totally appropriate to sentient isolate species, which have little group interaction. But they are insane beliefs to hold for a species as communal as the human species. This myth keeps humans in total ignorance of their true nature.

Earth is dominated by a species that cannot survive without intense repeated social contact and group support. Yet this same instinctual need is condemned.

So they repress that awareness and propagate a fiction that they are independent. They create cultural heroes who embody unattainable levels of emotional control, independence, and sexual attractiveness. They go to indoctrination sessions (called "movies" and "television") where they are taught to admire antisocial outlaws who live in constant danger, yet never cry, need others, or act terrified. Antidependence is the mark of heroism.

Then they leave these propaganda sessions and go back

to work. At work, every word and act is closely scrutinized, and nonconformists are ostracized. They are continually being severely instructed in how to comply with group demands.

They are forced to conform to a strict code of conduct in a very rigid and merciless environment. Yet after work, their personalities are encouraged to identify with characterizations of autonomy, lawlessness, and personal freedom. If they behaved like that at work, they would soon be exiled.

Often these contradictions create so much internal pressure that workers have to medicate themselves through the use of psychoactive chemicals, sometimes to the point of stupor and unconsciousness. It is easy for them to become addicted to these substances. Of course they are then judged by their society as morally deficient or psychologically immature, since they are depending on a substance, and any dependence is bad.

Zog's insights apply directly to your recovery. They explain why the combination of Twelve Step programs and psychological treatment is so much more effective in treating addictions than psychotherapy alone. Individual therapy is a lonely enterprise. It aggravates that myth of autonomy (I can do it all by myself!). In contrast, an AA meeting is one of those rare places where people congregate to heal each other, rather than to dominate, exploit, or control each other.

Recovery undoes centuries-old beliefs that place values of independence over values of interconnectedness. The myth of autonomy is shattered in AA. We discover that there are things we could never do alone. Yet, with the support, strength, and love of our group, they become possible.

Shame and Guilt Relievers

Recovery stretches beyond abstinence. To reenter life as a sober and fully alive person, you need to heal the interpersonal wounds that you inflicted upon yourself and upon others during the time you were lost in your addiction. This is what I call the interpersonal phase of recovery.

Psychotherapy can help you discover the roots of some of these wounds and heal them. The Twelve Steps can teach you the skills for cleaning up the messes you made, so you can start afresh. Steps Four through Nine deal specifically with repairing ripped relationships and learning the skills you need to avoid making the same mistakes again.

Step Four. Made a searching and fearless moral inventory of ourselves.

Step Five. Admitted to God, to ourselves, and to another human being the exact nature of our wrongs.

Step Six. Were entirely ready to have God remove all these defects of character.

Step Seven. Humbly asked God to remove our shortcomings.

Step Eight. Made a list of all persons we had harmed, and became willing to make amends to them all.

Step Nine. Made direct amends to such people wherever possible, except when to do so would injure them or others.

These are the shame-and-guilt-reliever Steps. Guilt and shame are natural healthy human emotions. Guilt is about doing. Guilt is a painful recognition that we did something that hurt someone else, or did something that tore at the fabric of civilized rules for living. Shame is about being. Shame is a painful recognition that a part of our basic nature is deficient, immature, or underdeveloped in comparison with others.

Neurotic guilt and shame do not move toward reparation and healing. They stay stuck in self-hatred and self-attack. They point us on a road back to using drugs and alcohol.

The difference between neurotic shame and healthy shame is the difference between humiliation and humility. Neurotic shame attacks you for your very nature. You are fat, ugly, weak, inferior, poor, stupid, crazy, or a loser. We have all heard these Inner Judge messages before.

Healthy shame is the awareness that we have some real limitations. It goes hand in hand with compassion and forgiveness. We will hurt the ones we love, no matter how hard we try not to. We will fail at times. We will disappoint others and ourselves. We are not perfect. We were all born with some capacities above normal, and we were all born retarded in some areas. As we age, we lose some capacities.

This is the human condition. Healthy shame is our encounter with these limitations. Healthy shame dissolves illusions of superiority. We are no longer free to judge because we have seen our imperfections. As the comic strip character Pogo put it, "We have met the enemy, and he is us."

This shame can open our heart to the imperfection of us all and lead us to a deeper, more compassionate connection with our fellow human beings on this planet. We are all doing the best we can with the hands we have been dealt.

Steps Four through Seven are a direct confrontation with our limitations and imperfections. They provide a

disciplined set of activities that support an honest confrontation of your own human frailties. This results in a
shift from toxic shame to healthy shame. The humility
that naturally arises from going through this process will
leave you less judgmental of your co-workers, and more
accepting and understanding of their foibles.

Steps Eight and Nine teach a technique for harnessing
healthy guilt in a creative and positive way. Healthy guilt
reminds us of our excessive egocentricity. We feel guilty
when we see how we have hurt others, often inadvertently, because we were wrapped up in ourselves. This
emotion hurts. That bad feeling can impel us to make
amends with that person. In this way the suffering of the
guilt is eased, and the breach between us and the person
we wounded is at least partially healed.

People who feel no guilt do not make amends and go
through life abusing others. Our guilt is a signal that we
have an empathetic heart. It is a gift in that it reminds us
that we have a shadow side and that we need to take
responsibility for the ones we hurt.

Making amends at work requires thoughtfulness. Too
often, in a desire to eradicate denial, recovering people
overdisclose and end up hurting themselves and others.
Don't be in a hurry with Step Nine.

It is better to work for years to save up money you
embezzled until you can repay it with interest, and then
make your amends, than it is to "'fess up" early in recovery and end up getting sent to prison. You and your family and loved ones must not be damaged in this process
of clearing your name. Get lots of advice from folks in the
program as you do this Step. Brainstorm every amend to
make sure you are not unintentionally creating more suffering for you or for others.

As we clean out our reservoir of old guilt and shame by

making amends, we become freer to interact openly with others around us. As we learn to make amends, we learn to forgive ourselves for not being perfect. We will never be perfect. If we are not perfect, then we can go ahead and make mistakes, because the technique of amends will enable us to clean up after our own messes.

CHAPTER EIGHT

The Balancing Act

How can we balance work, recovery, home, service, friendship, community, romance, family, fun, and rest? In today's world the pace seems to be getting faster and more frenetic. Faxes, cell phones, e-mail, portable TVs—we are working while we commute to work and are never out of touch with the rest of the globe. We want more, we want it all, we want it faster, and we want it right now! And your boss wants it right now, too! Time is money!

Recovery just makes matters worse. An already overbooked life now has to make room for meetings, recovery literature, individual therapy, group therapy, couples' work, recovery-oriented service work, daily meditation, and a healthy lifestyle. It seems exhausting. Trying to fit in all the recovery-related stuff just highlights how out of control your life feels.

It can become overwhelming. We need to begin to take charge of our lives, instead of being jerked around by all the bright lights, loud noises, and urgent deadlines. But before we can bring some order to the chaos of our lives, we need to examine the whole question of what balance really is. This chapter seeks to correct some myths about bringing balance to one's life. Dennis, one of the most unconventional clients I ever worked with, is the perfect spokesperson for revisioning balance.

Dennis's Story

Dennis was an unlikely candidate for therapy; I doubt he could sit still long enough for a session. His six-foot body was never still. A finger would be tapping or a foot vibrating; he was strung tight and always on the verge of explosive movement.

One-on-one, sit-down therapy was much too constraining. Recovery life coaching worked great for him. He could do it on his portable phone while he was working out on his exercise bike.

"If someone told me that recovery had anything to do with bringing balance into my life, I would have never walked through those doors. I was in line for the Olympic ski team in the downhill until I broke so many bones that I had to quit. When I found out I couldn't ski anymore, I got strung out for a while. Too many nights drinking and drugging myself to sleep. I took a dive till someone grabbed my arm and dragged me to a meeting. I cleaned out. Then, I got really restless.

"I couldn't stay still for a whole meeting, so I would go in and out of two or three a day, kind of averaging out as one whole meeting. I don't go for the God stuff at all. But it helps to know that a bunch of folks are rooting for me to stay straight and to get my yearly tokens. And it helps to have a place to talk about stuff I would otherwise bottle up.

"But sobriety was too boring. To survive, I had to take up free climbing and bouldering. I live for the edge. The phrase 'a balanced life' sends chills down my spine. It sounds like a nine-to-five job in a paisley tie and church on Sunday. Not for me!

"I own a wilderness supply store. I look for nice 'balanced' folks to run the floor, so I can take off for the mountains. But when I got a life coach to help me grow my business, he helped me see how critical balance really was for my work and for my recovery. Balance has nothing to do with boredom. It has everything to do with creating the time I need to push my limits."

For Dennis, balance is about living fully, passionately, and magnificently. For Riannon, balance brought another lesson.

Riannon's Story

"I was getting addicted to work. I knew it was an addiction because I was already two years clean and sober. I had learned to spot my chemical addictions and the cravings that went along with them. I was shocked to feel cravings to stay longer at work.

"I mean, it does make some sense. At home I had a grumpy eight-year-old son, a tired husband, and a dog who wanted to go for a walk. At work I was respected, listened to, and even looked up to. It was addicting to spend a half hour longer here and there, just to avoid walking through the door of my messy house.

"I love my husband and my son, don't get me wrong. And I was feeling guilty that I wanted to be at work, and not be home for them as a mother and a wife. But I was dreading the commute home more and more. And I was letting work-related projects creep into my weekends and evenings. I didn't want to become an absent parent, like my Dad was. And I didn't want to drift away from my husband. I knew I had to find a new balance between work and home."

Let's look at what balance isn't before we take a look at how to create it.

Myth #1: Balance has something to do with making all parts of your life equal. This view of balance has the image of a balance scale. The Inner Judge might say, "To bring true balance to your life, spend one-third of your life at work, one-third of your life involved with your personal life, and one-third asleep." Wrong! Balance has nothing to do with equality. A life lived in dynamic balance will have some activities taking up quite a bit of time and others making only rare appearances. Dennis knew that he had to honor his passion for excitement in order for his life to work. Riannon knew that balancing home and work had more to do with the quality of her life at home than the number of hours she spent there.

Myth #2: Creating balance in your life is learning to act like a grown-up. For some, balance can sound like imprisonment. These are people who enjoy life lived on the extremes, and many recovering folks fit into that description. "A balanced life" goes along with words like "responsible," "conservative," "mature," "sensible," and "old fogey."

For Dennis, it was easy to correct this image. His experience as a skier taught him about true balance. Balance is about keeping that perfect combination of risk and bare control that keeps you flying downhill, one moment away from a wipeout. It can't be done if safety and caution are the operating principles. It is a form of intense play.

For Riannon, her grown-up needs for respect and acknowledgment were getting met at work, but she had no idea how to get some of these needs met at home. She was stuck in the perspective that, at home, she took care of everyone else's needs and her needs were unimportant.

Myth #3: Balance is a destination. One can mistake balance for some static state of being. From this delusion, it appears that balance is a state to strive for. Once you get there, you can relax. Any skier, surfer, or mountain climber knows that view to be false. Balance is a dynamic process, not a steady state. Each moment asks for a new balance. Balance is a verb, a state of being. If you cling to the balance you had in the past, you are headed for a nasty fall!

In order to move to a place of balance in your life, you need to free yourself from some limiting perspectives about time. They go something like this: "There is never enough time. Time is running out. This is just the way it is, and I can't do anything about it. I have to do stuff I don't want to do, and by the time I get off work, and away from taking care of everyone else, I am too tired to do anything."

These are compelling perspectives. It's hard to step outside the box they create. But as long as you stay stuck in them, you will not be able to take full responsibility for your life. Until you can do that, you cannot change. (Much of the material on perspective that I'm presenting here comes from the book *Co-Active Coaching* by Laura Whitworth, Henry House, and Phil Sandahl [Davies-Black Publishing, 1998].)

Tool #1: Perspective Work (Worksheet 8–1)

Let's do some work in opening up the cramped space in you that determines how you relate to time. Write down the things you tell yourself about time. Some of them may be limiting beliefs you have about time. Make sure to include positive perspectives that you may hold, or may want to hold. Maybe a brand-new perspective on time might pop up. If your list goes to nine or ten, that's fine.

This was Dennis's list.

Perspectives about time

1. I want more of it.
2. Time is an illusion.
3. My time is not my own; other people call the shots.
4. Time is to be savored.
5. I don't know how to manage time.
6. Cram life into every minute.
7. I have too much time.
8. Time is an enemy.

Riannon's list read like this:

1. Everyone needs my time.
2. There's not enough of it.
3. My time is best served at work.
4. Time is running out.

Now it's your turn. Fill in the first column of worksheet 8–1.

Finished? Good job. Now take a moment and write next to each perspective how it feels when you are standing inside it. How does the world look from that perspective? Do you like it? Is it confining? What comes up for you when you are seeing the world from those eyes? Take the time to step into each perspective and look around, the hard ones as well as the easy ones.

Dennis wrote for his item #8, "Time is an enemy": "I have to live so hard, and time is on my heels, threatening to run out. It is scary and intense in this perspective, like a war between me and time."

Riannon wrote about her item #3, "My time is best served at work": "I know when I have successfully accomplished something at work. The project is finished. It's not like housecleaning, which never ends. Standing in this perspective feels great, like I make a difference."

Write down how your perspectives feel.

The hard part of using the perspective tool is the realization that any one of these beliefs is just a perspective. We are convinced that some beliefs are complete and total truth with no exceptions possible. We have lots of evidence to back up our position. Often our position is that the situation is hopeless and we are victims trapped in a tragedy we can do nothing about.

Notice how your feelings and thoughts changed as you moved from perspective to perspective. What if there were a lot more ways to view the situation than you had previously imagined? What if you could step into a perspective that wasn't so trapped?

Now choose a perspective, a belief, a position about time that would feel freer and more spacious. One that affirms your life.

Sit down in this perspective. Really put it on. Imagine that it is a room in your ideal house. What does it look like? How does it make you feel? Who do you have to be to live this perspective with all your heart? What is your world like from this perspective? At the bottom of the worksheet page write for a while about how your life changes from living in this perspective.

There are three lessons you need to learn to make sure that this perspective will be the one that brings balance into your life.

Lesson #1: The Rule of Three. We try to keep things simple. When we think of making choices in our lives, we tend to choose between two conflicting positions: either I finish this report by working overtime or I go to my AA meeting. Either I call my sponsor or I buy some dope. Either I read my daily meditation in the morning or I make it to work on time.

"Either-or" is actually the enemy of choice. It is the strategy of the Inner Judge, who wants to organize your life according to good-bad, right-wrong "shoulds."

You might have noticed when you used the perspective tool how choices and options opened up once we got beyond "either-or." So the rule of three is simple: you cannot freely choose from only two options. There are always more than two.

Dennis was very skeptical of this tool. He thought that he had to take a hard line with his addictions and that opening up the mind to choosing might leave him room to relapse. So I asked him to make up a list about using alcohol. Here is his list:

Perspectives on drinking
1. I can't drink or I will die.
2. I can handle my liquor.
3. Drinking is fun and I don't want to give it up.
4. Drinking makes me sick, in a lot of ways.
5. Drinking helps me get away from my pain.
6. Drinking brings me a lot of pain.
7. If I drink again I don't know if I have it in me to recover again.
8. I am happier sober.

He realized that he could choose sobriety for the quality of life it brings him, not just out of fear of blowing it.

Lesson #2: Every Yes Needs a No. To bring balance into your life, you will be saying yes to activities that make your life passionate, nurturing, interesting, clean, sober, and worth living. This means that you will have to say no to other activities and demands on your time.

We hate saying no to something we want. That's part of the impulsive, addictive mentality. We want it all. The problem is that wanting it all can backfire. When we see that we can't have it all, we can easily give up in hopelessness and settle for very little.

Creating balance in your life means carving out time for things that are essential to you. Make a Yes/No List (worksheet 8–2). For everything you say yes to in your life, look at the no's you will have to say to accomplish that. A section of Riannon's list looked like this:

Yes	No
Quality time being a Mom. . .	Taking on extra projects at work
	Spending most of my time at home doing housework
Noon AA/OA meetings	Working through lunch at my desk
	Socializing over lunch

Saying no affirms your capacity to choose. No is a muscle that needs development. Don't let a day go by without at least one hard no put out there. Here is some homework for today: say no four times in the next two hours. See what comes up when you do that.

Lesson #3: Choose Guilt. I am guessing that the following little Inner Judge voice might have come up sometime during the time you did those exercises. It might have said something like, "Yeah, but I can't do that. That's selfish. It would hurt someone's feelings, or let someone down, or make someone angry." Along with that thought came a twinge of guilt.

Guess what? Guilt is unavoidable. It will come up whenever you assert your will and desire in the face of inconveniencing someone else. Codependency rules when you feel like you cannot endure living with that guilt. You will be unable to create balance in your life until you build up your capacity to breathe into your guilt, feel the pain of it, and choose for yourself anyway.

Often the choice is between guilt and resentment. If you take care of yourself, you will feel bad about not taking care of other people (guilt). If you take care of other people at the expense of taking care of yourself, you will eventually resent them. Since you are going to feel lousy either way, when in doubt choose guilt. Guilt can be relieved; resentment just festers until it explodes in attack or implodes in a relapse.

Guilt is information. It informs you that your actions impact others. And you may have to make amends, knowing that you are choosing for yourself instead of choosing to take care of someone else.

Guilt is also sometimes wise and sometimes foolish. Take a close look at each feeling of guilt to see if it is guidance or self-attack. You have to make a lot of mistakes on the way toward balance. You will hurt others unnecessarily. You will think you are acting in your best interests and end up seeing that you were just being arrogant. Recovery involves a lot of falling flat on your face. Eventually you will learn to appreciate the many failures it takes to learn new behavior.

I will let Riannon end this chapter:

"I realized that everything important in my life would have to change if I were going to bring my life into balance. So I started making unbreakable dates with my husband. And I left work behind me when I walked out of the office, and stopped bringing a briefcase full of papers home with me.

"And we got a cleaning lady once every two weeks. When the maid service came, I would go out with my son on an adventure, while she cleaned the house. I still feel like I spend too much time at work. That may not change any time soon. But the quality of my life both at work and at home is a lot better."

PART THREE

Ongoing Recovery

Riding the Waves

■

CHAPTER NINE

Library Resource Center
Renton Technical College
3000 NE 4th St.
Renton, WA 98056-4195

Burning Out

In 1982, Christina Maslach published *Burnout: The High Cost of Caring*. Since then, the term has become part of the language of work. Extensive studies have outlined the nature of burnout.

Burnout is characterized by feelings of exhaustion, depletion, emptiness, cynicism, hopelessness, and being trapped, blocked, or weighted down. It is implicated in increased levels of illness, accidents, addictions, absenteeism, resignations, and firings. It was first identified in people who had a high degree of frustrating contact with others on the job: social workers, police officers, salespeople, and so on.

Later research revealed that burnout is more pervasive and can occur in many job situations where workers feel powerless to change their circumstances and overwhelmed with the workload.

Often episodes of burnout occur when something is added to an already stressful load. A pet dies or you have a minor accident, and all of a sudden you are filled with bitterness and resentment, or your whole life seems pointless and meaningless. The old you starts to crack.

Traditional psychology has looked for all sorts of roots

to the problem of burnout. The causes of burnout have often been identified in the structure of the work setting itself, rather than blaming the workers for their suffering. This perspective lifted the load of guilt off the victim of burnout. However, psychological research has done little to reduce burnout in the workplace.

The field of addiction treatment can make a substantial contribution to the study of workplace burnout. People in recovery from addiction also experience burnout, but there is a different name for it. Most people who are at least a year into sobriety know about a phenomenon called the "dry drunk." Characteristics of a dry drunk include depression, testiness, increased isolation, low self-esteem, anxiety, addictive behavior, increased cravings, sleep disturbance, physical illness (flulike symptoms), and feeling out of control of one's emotional state. Janet can describe it from the inside.

 ### Janet's Story

Janet became my coaching client when she went through the two-year anniversary dry drunk. She worked with me a year, and had another, less intense period of "recovery hangover," but by then she knew it for what it was and rode it through without too much difficulty.

"I thought they were kidding about the two-year blues. My sponsor warned me that it could happen. She said that I would feel like I was back in my first week of recovery. But I didn't listen to her. I thought if I could make it past a year, I'd be on Easy Street!

"Well, I am in it now. It feels like I was up all night last night partying, even though I went to bed totally clean at 9:30. I am depressed. I wonder, 'What's the use of all this recovery, if it ends up with me feeling this lousy?'

"I work in a residential treatment center as a counselor to emotionally disturbed kids. These days it feels like putting Band-Aids on cancer. No one is getting any better, and work feels totally pointless, a real professional dead end. At home, my relationship with my lover seems headed down the tubes. My whole life is crap. I just don't get it."

Addiction treatment views the dry drunk as an expected phase in a successful recovery. The goal is not to eliminate it but to manage its inevitable appearance. There are such strong parallels between burnout and dry drunks that the same interventions may work for both. Following are some perspectives to support healthy management of these periods.

Nonblaming

Nonblaming means not attacking anyone. To talk about victims of burnout perpetrates a perspective that says there are victims, victimizers, and powerlessness. Not the powerlessness of surrender, a powerful personal choice, but the powerlessness of being at the mercy of others.

A brilliant model called the Karpman Drama Triangle was developed in the 1970s. Much codependency work utilized it. It looks like this:

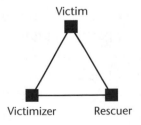

It is a picture of how victimization and pathological care-taking weave together in an inescapable prison. You can start at any corner.

Say you woke up this morning, went to brush your teeth, and discovered that your partner left the cap off the toothpaste. Now, you have had many talks about how this upsets you. Yet your partner keeps doing it. You know that this is more than just carelessness. This is a symptom of the callous, selfish, and unloving way you get treated by this person whom you love so unselfishly. Welcome to the victim corner.

When you try to share your feelings, really working not to express the intensity of the anger and betrayal you feel (even though a little seeps out), your partner erupts in unreasonable anger, blasts you for carping all the time, and stalks off to work. That way your partner gets to explore the victimizer role.

You run over to the phone and call your best friend to tell all about the way you are being treated. Your friend may totally align with you and join you in judging the hell out of your partner. Then he or she gets to play rescuer.

But wait, it gets even more interesting. Later that day your partner calls to tell you how her or his feelings were hurt by the angry way you reacted. You hang up. You get to play victimizer.

Your best friend calls to dump some more on your partner, and you realize how this person is driving a wedge between you and your true love. You hang up again.

You get scared your partner might leave you. Then you call your partner and apologize and soothe over any hurt feelings. It is caretaker (rescuer) time. Then you talk about how you have come to realize that it's your best friend who is causing most of the tension between the two of you. You and your partner go on to judge and criticize your former best friend.

Or let's look at work. You're sitting at your desk, minding your own business, and your boss dumps a report on your desk, one you worked hard on. "This is unacceptable. Rework sections three and four."

"How dare he!" (Victim.) "I'll show him, I'll quit!" (Victimizer.) "Did you see that? Isn't he the worst pig you've ever had to work for?" (Manipulating a co-worker to be your rescuer.)

We take all these roles and can switch from victim to victimizer to rescuer at the drop of a toothpaste cap. There is only one exit from this racetrack.

To get out of the game you must choose to stand in the victimizer role. Most of the game is spent trying to avoid that corner, or grasping it with righteous self-justification. But it is a hot place to stay in, and an even harder place to consciously choose.

You stand in that corner, but not from anger. You stand there and bravely tell your truth about your experience. You do not blame, or attack, or twist the knife. You do not attack yourself, sell yourself out, or self-deprecate. You just say what is true for you. "I get frustrated when you don't do what I want you to do, like put the cap on the toothpaste." "I don't mind reworking those sections, but I didn't appreciate you telling me it was unacceptable. I worked hard on that report and I needed my work acknowledged."

Doing that usually irritates blamers. They come at you, expecting you either to attack them or to join them in blaming someone else. When you don't play that game, eventually they tire and go off to play the blame game with someone else.

In a burned-out state it is easy to believe that many

other people are directly responsible for your suffering. You will only let go of that perspective after seeing that it doesn't make the situation any better, no matter how true it may appear to be.

It is also true that it's not all your fault. There is an expression I've heard at meetings: the problem isn't that I'm a miserable worm, and the problem isn't that I think I'm so very special. The problem is that I think I'm a very special worm. Or put more graphically, I'm a piece of shit and the world revolves around me.

Letting go of the identification with being the problem is one of the hardest tasks to do in achieving a nonblaming mindset. If anyone said to our kids or our parents half the things we regularly say to ourselves, we would lay waste to their planet. But we call ourselves these awful names as a matter of habit. Sometimes we even tell ourselves that we are doing it for our own good.

Nonblaming is a radical act. It lies at the heart of healing the wound of burnout. It comes from a sincere desire to end the suffering you and those around you are enduring. When you get to that point, grace can occur, and you find a way to live with that, something that felt untenable just a little while ago.

Dialogue

The voice within you that's burned out is shrill. Sometimes caustic, sometimes bitter, often bone weary, this voice commands your attention. It requires a sense of balance to work with it. Shove it away, and sooner or later it will seek retribution. This can come in the form of illness, depression, addictive acting out, and other forms of self-destructive or self-weakening behaviors.

Hand this burned-out voice the car keys and you might

quit, dump your partner, move to Timbuktu, and start the cycle all over again. The skill is in inviting this voice to the bargaining table to speak and be heard, but not to dominate the conversation.

Have a family meeting with yourself. Place all your inner voices around the table. Let in the stern dad, the gentle mom (or vice versa). Be sure that the little kid and the wise old person get airtime. Bring burnout in, too. Remember that your role is to moderate and make sure no one voice runs the show. Don't feel that this meeting is for the purpose of making any decisions. It is just to give all sides of you a chance to speak. Keep this conversation going, and the right decision, if any is needed, will naturally emerge.

Aim Low

Burnout often occurs when you are working with very large projects. Welfare workers working with poverty, air traffic controllers holding thousands of lives in their hands, and even Janet and her cottage of children all face huge challenges. Janet can tell you about aiming low:

"One of the big things that helped me crawl out of my burnout hole was to get realistic. I went into the job expecting that I would save these kids from their mental illness, their dysfunctional families, and their stressful economic situations. Well, I didn't really say those words to myself, but some idealistic naive part believed that. When that didn't happen, it sometimes broke my heart. Worse, I began feeling like a failure.

"With the help of some co-workers, and your coaching, I came to accept the power of the limited impact I could have on these kids. Within my cottage walls, I could give them the experience of being loved, respected, and cared about. I have no idea how much of that stuck. It's really none of my business. The results of what I do are in the hands of a Higher Power.

"But I was responsible for the way I interacted with them today. By cutting my responsibility down to manageable, bite-sized pieces, I could feel good at the end of the day, even if some kid that I really liked blew out and had to go to Juvie. I still know I gave my best to all of them."

Letting Go

We know how hard letting go is in recovery. And we know how essential it is. But work gives us a whole new set of challenges around the issue of control, as Allison can attest to:

Allison's Story

"My drinking was pretty pathetic. Every morning I would wake up with a new resolve. 'Today, I will not have any beer after work.' Every evening that would fly out the window, and I would have one, or many. I felt so crappy about myself. The next morning, I swore to myself, 'Today will really be different!' I was completely out of control.

"Nothing changed, until my new lover told me I had a drinking problem. I knew it all along, but the crowd I drank with told me I was neurotic to think there was anything wrong. It was such a relief to hear the truth. I stopped soon after that.

"Now, it's a year and a half later, and I realize the same pattern has come back, but it has nothing to do with drinking. I am a salesperson. I am successful only if I continually prospect for new clients. When I stop prospecting, I shut off the pipeline. Three months down the road, I will be out of business. I know this like I know my own name.

"Every morning I wake up, swearing that, 'Today, I am going to put in at least three hours on the phone, cold calling!' At the end of the day, I look back, and see I have had a great time talking with all my friends at the office. I put out all the fires that happened with the accounts that I have open. I never made one cold call. 'Tomorrow,' I vow, 'I am really going at it!' A few weeks of those days pile up, and suddenly I realize, 'It's exactly the same as my drinking!' Once again, I am totally out of control!

"It's so frustrating. It is affecting my business. I get really depressed about it. Am I broken? I'm giving up hope."

Letting Go of Control

Out of control. Over control. Controlled drinking. "Get in control!" Control permeates every aspect of addiction and recovery. Trying to control a behavior results in repeated confrontations with the truth that we are out of control.

We discover in recovery that acknowledging we are out of control makes room for change. Letting go of harsh control over our feelings allows tears, anger, guilt, shame, joy, gratitude, and healing to occur. Surrendering control, be it to a mentor, a sponsor, a group, a program, or a Higher Power, leads to relief from the need to control. Paradoxes around control abound.

At work it seems all that we learn in recovery is reversed. We have to control our inventory, control our costs, control our customers, and always control our emotions. Work is serious business, and no place for uncontrolled emotional outbursts. How can we negotiate our way through these two conflicting perspectives?

No new technology here, just the Serenity Prayer: "God grant me the serenity to accept the things I cannot change, the courage to change the things I can, and the wisdom to know the difference." Looking closely at it, we see how it provides the path through this mess.

It opens with the word "God." This is a tough concept for many to swallow in our secular society. It is especially hard to address in the antireligious world of work. The early founders of AA knew about this antitheism and included in their Big Book a chapter "To the Agnostic." Conventional wisdom in meetings insists that it doesn't matter what you believe in, as long as you believe in something larger than your personality.

The issue comes back to control. As long as you are alone, you must control your impulses. However, once you see yourself as a part of something larger that you can trust—a group, a movement, a family, a community, a theology—then you may loosen the grip on control and know that you are held safely in a larger container.

Define God as something that is larger than yourself and that cares about you. This can get folks over the "God" stumbling block. Sometimes even work can fit that description. I have had a number of clients who owe their sobriety to bosses who wouldn't give up on them and wouldn't indulge them.

The next phrase is asking for the serenity to accept what you cannot influence. This deals with the difference between hopelessness and acceptance. Behavioral psychology has done research with animals from dogs to humans demonstrating the importance of this principle. They call it "learned helplessness" and believe it has a lot to do with depression.

In one famous experiment Martin Seligman had an electric pad completely carpeting an enclosure. He would then put dogs in it and shock them, and they could not escape. After a while the dogs would just lie down and take it. Then the experimenter would open a half door to a cage that had no electric carpet. All the dogs had to do was jump over a low barrier.

The dogs wouldn't do it. They had resigned themselves to being shocked. Offering food, calling them—nothing worked. Finally the experimenter tied ropes around their necks and pulled them over the fence. Sometimes it took over thirty pulling sessions before the dogs learned that they could now escape the shock by jumping the barrier.

We can sink into that same sort of resigned feeling of "no exit." If you believe that you are alone and there is nothing in life but one electrified carpet after another, you give up. This is not acceptance; it is resignation and burnout.

The way out begins when you see that you are not alone. Then you see others very much like you who are not despairing. Instead they are doing what they can, and hanging with the rest. You begin to learn that you too might be able to jump over the barrier. You can accept the stuff you didn't create, because you know sooner or later that it will change or you will move on to something better.

Then comes the piece about courage to make the changes you can. We call it the Serenity Prayer, but I think it should be called the Courage Prayer. Taking skillful action, jumping over the fence, is the key to learning the lesson of control. The goal in skillful control is understanding the concept of limited control. We have enough courage and control to not take a hit of marijuana right now. We may not have enough control to swear off toking for a month. So we don't worry about it. We just focus on right now. All we need is limited control. Courage gives us the strength to apply what limited control we have.

Courage happens all the time in the workplace, as does cowardice and waiting. Courage speaks against injustice and for creativity, innovation, discipline, and common sense. To learn skillful courage is to learn to fight the important fights and let go of the irrelevant, petty, or unimportant fights. We learn to let go of the fights that may be important to someone else, but not to us. We choose when and where to engage, not out of reaction, but consciously and with care to maintain self-respect. We focus the warrior within us, leash her when necessary, and let her loose when needed.

Wisdom, the final request of the prayer, comes only from making many glorious mistakes. There are no short-cuts to wisdom. To get there you must forgive yourself again and again, as you fall down on the way to learning to walk. Maybe we should also pray for "the compassion to forgive myself as I make the mistakes that will give me the wisdom to know the difference."

Vacations

Vacations can be lifesavers, and they can be total disasters. They can provide a break from job stress, a rest and recuperation period. They can also provide some new life experiences that enliven your regular life. But they are not the cure for burnout. Burnout is healed on the job.

For you to create the space for a vacation to nurture you, you need to leave work. This is much harder to do energetically than it is to do geographically. Work-related thoughts continually push to center stage, even at three o'clock in the morning. Sometimes we drank and did drugs just to get rid of this torturous obsessing. Janet told me how a co-worker got free.

"One day I was just spacing out, and I noticed Pat driving away from work. When she got to the gate the car stopped for about a minute. Then she drove on. The next night I noticed that she did the same thing. Finally I had to ask, 'Pat, what do you do when you drive home at night?'

'I have been working in this cottage for fifteen years,' she replied. 'I had to find a way to make this job manageable, and it sure wasn't going to be by making it any less stressful. Instead, I decided that I needed a refuge. So every day after work, I stop by the entrance and ceremoniously dump my load of thoughts, feelings worries, concerns, and stresses that are focused on work stuff. Then I drive on, free. You didn't notice, but I pause when I come in through that entrance in the mornings, too. I pick up the load that I've left there, and start thinking about work again. It may seem silly, but I have been here longer than any other staff, so I guess it works.'"

Pat knew how to make every day a vacation, but some jobs require a permanent vacation. The fit between you and the job may just be unattainable. No blame. It is neither your fault nor the job's fault. Just a bad fit. Make sure you take your time in making that decision. If you wait long enough, you might change enough to find a way to make it work.

Leaving one job may be brilliant. Leaving seven jobs in three years may be a problem. The only concern is if you find that in sobriety you have a long string of job failures. To reverse that may require some professional help.

The Inward Path

We have looked at some perspectives on burnout. We have looked on it as a part of the Karpman Drama Triangle. We have imagined it as an inner voice. We have seen it as a result of unrealistic expectations. We tried on the perspective that it was a resistance to surrender and trust, and also considered that it was caused, in part, by an overly hard focus on work. Now we turn to a perspective that burnout may be a natural part of the growth cycle. Some cross-discipline research suggests that the regression periods that recovering folks call dry drunks are not unique to addiction recovery.

Patients recovering from intensive surgery and cancer also go through predictable low periods at one month, three months, six months, nine months, one year, two years, five years, and nine years. This may be a part of the healing cycle.

In any life, there are major challenges to the stability of our personality: illness, recovery, marriage, divorce, getting a new job, and getting fired from your old one. In order to make it through these trials, old internal mental structures will have to crumble and new ones take their place. This is a painful process.

What if some instances of burnout/dry drunk/regression periods are a natural element whenever someone faces a major identity change? The depression and exhaustion may be a natural by-product of the personality going through major rewiring. As you integrate the new dimensions of your personality, the low periods come further and further apart.

This is a nonblaming perspective. The person experiencing burnout is not at fault. The work site is not at fault. But both the individual and the environment can become more skillful at addressing the natural stresses of the job. The individual and the organization can work together so that stresses do not become debilitating.

There are things an individual can do and things a work

setting can do. This chapter's focus is on individual tools. Chapter 13 shows a boss using some tools for changing the workplace.

What can you do? Personal growth moves you out of burnout. Recovery life coaching, a community of honest friends, service work, psychotherapy, vision quests, and growth workshops all help kick start the stagnant mind. Perhaps the abuse, insensitivity, lack of appreciation, and paltry rewards you perceive outside of you also reflect a bleak, decaying inner world. As Shakespeare put it, "The fault, dear Brutus, is not in our stars, but in ourselves." Do the hard work of facing those projections, so that you know which battles are worth fighting and which may be shadow projections of your own imbalance.

Remember that all growth spirals through the dark lands and the light. The sense of total depletion and emptiness may be the necessary precursor to renewal. Be gentle, know that this too shall pass, and as Jennifer Stone, a writer and wise commentator on the human condition, puts it, "Go easy, and if you can't go easy, go as easy as you can."

CHAPTER TEN

Dare to Dream Again

Larry's Story

 Larry slumped into my consulting room. His hair was wild. His eyes had dark shadows under them. His clothes were rumpled. He collapsed into the chair and sighed. He was six months into recovery from alcoholism and going downhill fast. In his first session with me, he complained about work.

"I was a dreamer when I went into recovery. I dreamed of running my own retreat center, where people having emotional difficulties could come for a healing rest. I dreamed of being a professor in an ivy-covered university. I dreamed of being a best-selling author. I dreamed of exotic women.

"But when I wasn't dreaming, I was judging myself. I really didn't like what I saw. I was a thirty-six-year-old audio salesman at a discount electronics store. I was wandering through my life without much direction or passion.

"When I was drinking I had an excuse. I would vow, 'Tomorrow I am really going to get it together!' Feeling a new resolve, I would go out for my evening exercise, a brisk jog to 'Cafe Depresso' to drink a liter of white wine.

When tomorrow came I had to manage my hangover, and thoughts about sculpting my future were in the trash can."

Larry's first few sessions were focused on his painful depression. He consulted with a psychiatrist and got on an antidepressant. This had a huge positive impact on his moods and on his appearance. But he still could not get focused on his work.

In our counseling he uncovered a buried passion. He had always wanted to write, but his Inner Judge had convinced him that becoming a writer was an unrealistic and naive goal. The Judge was dead wrong. In helping me write this chapter he remembered that first session:

"I told you, that first day, that I was a dreamer. Today, I have seven years of recovery. I am still a dreamer. Sometimes, I dream just for the fun of it. But other times I dream in order to create. The big dreams grab me and possess me. I channel them into reality.

"I write every day. It is my central passion. Midnight often finds me in front of my computer screen. I catch dreams, wrap words around them, and pour them into books for others to relish.

"Without recovery, I would still be wandering, and hoping. With recovery, antidepressants, and a little help from my friends, my dreams have become my work."

Larry has written five mystery novels and is hard at work on his first mainstream novel. He is deeply grateful for his life and his recovery.

Larry began lost. The same wasn't true for Julie. Julie knew exactly what she wanted. Yet she had to travel many of the same roads that Larry did.

Julie's Story

"I was the weirdo in high school. I was a girl, and a hacker. My friends called me Nerdella and gave me tons of grief. Tough. I loved messing with computer programs, and I was damn good at it. In college I also messed with coke, meth, and Stoli (vodka). Perfect drugs for programming into the dawn. I got a job that would support my habit, and all was well till I crashed and barricaded myself in my room, terrified to leave the house. That stuff rots your mind.

"I always knew what I wanted to do. I read cyberpunk when I was ten. Artificial intelligence. My passion. When I crawled into recovery I realized that I had sold my programming talents to the highest bidder to support my habit. If I was going to be clean and sober, by God I was going to work in the field that I loved.

"It wasn't that easy. On the way I had picked up a lot of baggage in my head about how I had blown my chances and how I was just a hack programmer. I felt my brain had been snorted up my nose, and there was not enough left to do what I wanted to do. I knew it was too late.

"I had a lot of reprogramming to do on myself. In fact, I needed a whole new operating system. Meetings, sponsors, counselors, friends, and regular meditation helped me erase the viruses of self-hate and negative thinking. Or at least get them to shut up a little. Then I had to envision what I wanted and implement a plan for getting it."

Julie is now a lead programmer for a project working with robotics and artificial intelligence in medicine.

There are five essential factors needed for the journey that both Larry and Julie took from seeing themselves as passive victims of fate to knowing that they are powerful players and cocreators of their destinies. The factors that allow you to move from dream into manifestation are belief, vision, planning, habit, and support.

Belief

The first step is to hold the belief that you actually can change. What keeps you from this belief is the Inner Judge, all your internal judgments, criticisms, and negative pictures you hold of yourself. They seem so true. It is hard, at first to notice that these are just transient, internal, negative voices.

But as you practice "surfing" your cravings, you can also practice "surfing" your messages of self-hatred and judgment. They too have a trigger, a climax, and a falling-off phase.

A belief is a conviction that something is true. Before recovery you may have been convinced that you were weak, or selfish, or evil, or maybe just inferior. You were also convinced that you couldn't stop drinking or using drugs. Oh, sure, you would start out with a resolution, but your conviction that your craving was stronger than you always won out.

Now you are discovering that, while you still may have cravings, you also have the support, both inside you and outside of you, to weather those cravings, one day at a time. So maybe some of those other beliefs are false also. The following tool, which may remind you of the Denial Destroyer, might help.

Tool: The Belief Deconstructor (Worksheet 10–1)

Wait until the next time you're having an Inner Judge storm, when you are utterly convinced that you're bad, wrong, and awful. Then write down the list of all the things you're saying about yourself. Leave some room after each item. When you're done, put the list away. You might notice a little lifting of the cloud cover just by doing this.

Later, on a day when you are feeling pretty good about yourself, pull out that list. Under each item, write a retraction, clarification, or answer to that accusation.

One of Larry's Deconstructors looked like this: "I am so weak. I am a greedy pig, and eat anything I want, and am just getting fatter and fatter!" he had written on a bad day. Later he wrote in response: "Not true: There are times when I go unconscious about my food, and eat for the medication of it. Those times are getting fewer and fewer. I am eating healthy five or six days a week, which is healthier eating than I have ever done before."

The *next* time your Inner Judge trots out a repetition of its incorrect belief or accusation, pull out the Deconstructor, read the truth to yourself, and then send your Judge away on a one-way cruise to Antarctica. You are replacing false beliefs about yourself with the truth.

Vision

A powerful, passionate vision is unstoppable! A detailed picture of your dream will pull you toward it. To create such a vision requires imagination, creativity, and, most of all, courage.

One day some part of you had a vision that you could be free from enslavement to your addictions. It might have started with a fragile spark of hope. But that was all your vision needed. You took your first step toward recovery.

On the way you might have fallen often. You might have awakened on many mornings wondering if it was worth it, or if you could do it one more day. But you kept moving toward your vision, even when all felt lost.

That is how powerful vision is. Imagine your life if every aspect of it was inspired by vision. It is not about making your life perfect; it is about making your life delicious.

The gratitude that you have discovered in recovery makes a perfect foundation for building your entire life based on your vision. The house you build on that foundation needs to have the support of your voice. A vision statement puts your inspiration into words that can lead you toward it. An unwritten vision is just a good idea. But a vision document holds you accountable to yourself to see that it becomes a reality. Following are some suggestions to help you write your vision statement (worksheet 10–2):

1. Determine the territory. Your recovery is central to your vision. And there are some other areas of your life that also need some visionary attention. For instance:

- your physical body (health, fitness, appearance)
- your environment (home, office, car)
- your relationships (family, lover, life partner, work, church, community, old friends, and others)
- your spiritual and philosophical life (your source of meaning)
- your personal growth and mental health
- your career (vocation, money management, retirement)
- your recreational life

This is just a list of possible areas. Customize this list to fit the important areas of your life.

2. Step into the future. The following is a short guided imagery exercise, like the one you did to find your cloak in chapter 3. You need a quiet place to either read this to yourself or record it so you can close your eyes and follow the words.

> Begin by feeling your breath. Watch as it slows and deepens. Follow your breath as you draw it into your lungs. Imagine that you draw it deeper and deeper into your belly with each breath....
>
> Now imagine the television set of your mind gently glowing. As you look closer you can see that it is a new program called "This Will Be Your Life." You see that this show is about you, ten years from now. It begins with some scenes from your early years. Notice which scenes come on the screen....Then it shows you as you are this year. Again see what important images from the past twelve months come on the screen....Now it cuts to a scene of you ten years from now, speaking directly to you today. Your future self is telling you today about what your life is like, what you do for money, whom you are with, where you live, and what you do with your time. Listen and watch carefully as your future self shows you scenes of your life ten years hence....Now the show is over, and the glow dies, and you return to an awareness of your breath and your body. You are awakening refreshed and aware of everything you saw and heard.

Write down your experience. Now, from your list and from your experience in front of your internal TV, begin to write your vision.

3. Write your vision. Some helpful hints for vision writing:

- Write as though it has already happened. In this way it pulls you toward it. Writing "I am a highly successful saleswoman, and I win the top sales award in my office every year" is more powerful than "I want to win top awards in sales" or "I am going to win Salesperson of the Year."
- Don't pull your punches. Look at the difference between "I will try to lose ten pounds" and "I am slim, at my desired weight of 134."
- Be specific. State ambitious goals that you can measure and be proud of. "I save for retirement" is not half as clear as "I put fifteen thousand dollars a year into my retirement accounts."
- Include all areas of your life.
- Ask yourself, "For the sake of what?" Then state what your purpose on this planet in this lifetime is all about. Be bold.

This is Larry's vision statement:

I write because it is how I give back my gift of life and of recovery. I write at least three books a year. I publish at least three books a year. I make a six-figure salary. I do not create unsecured debt. I appear on the *New York Times* Best Seller List at least once a year. I deepen my relationship with my wife, my son, my brother, and my mom. I lead a balanced and healthy life, meditating and praying, dieting, and working out at least four days each week. I do at least two hours of service work weekly and attend my home group and at least one other group weekly. I act as a model for those new to recovery, while never forgetting to be humble and grateful for the gifts it gives me. I love my life.

Julie's vision reads:

I am alive and successful in all areas of my life. I am breaking new ground in the area of co-vergent decision-making subroutines in microprocessors. My co-workers trust me and appreciate the quality of my work. I deserve the respect I get at work and am left alone to follow my passions. I am in vibrant good health. I have a great relationship and never have to worry about money.

Planning (Worksheet 10–3)

For a vision statement to pull you toward it, you need to show up. This means you need to move from the broad scope of the vision all the way down to the minute detail of its implementation. As Stephen Covey, author of *Seven Habits of Highly Effective People,* points out, now you can begin with the end in mind. You know where you are going. All you have to do is work backward toward your present life.

In deciding what steps you need to take, remember that each step must be specific, measurable, ambitious, and something about which you can take action. The vision worksheet (worksheet 10–2) will be helpful.

Larry defined eight goals from his vision statement and made up monthly sheets on each of them.

This is a page from Larry's monthly plan:

Planning for the month of _February_

Visionary Goal: _I write three books a year_

List the projects that need to be accomplished to meet that goal, with completion date:

1. _Club Wicked completed 4/30/99 (done)_
2. _A Lost and Lonely Man completed by 7/1/99 (done)_
3. _Landing on Four Feet completed by 12/15/99_

This month's target for each of these projects, with completion date:

1. _Send first five chapters of Club Wicked to Laura for copyediting (2/27)_
2. _A Lost and Lonely Man—flesh out back story on Victor (2/21)_
3. _Landing on Our Feet—research coffee plantation life in Columbia in 1980s (2/14)_

On the first of each month, schedule into your daily planner time to work on projects.

Larry knew that he alone was personally responsible for achieving each milestone. He also knew that, without a structure around him, it would be easy to forget these goals as he got caught up in the daily drama of life. That is why he used the suggestions to make the first of every month a day to schedule time for working on his projects, before he booked in anyone else.

Habit

Vision becomes a way of life when one automatically does what is needed. In the beginning we act, in part, because we "should" do it. We should diet and exercise. We should read the Big Book every morning. All very good ideas that support our recovery. All ideas that have not yet been grounded into habit.

Good ideas require quite a lot of willpower to practice in a regular disciplined fashion. Willpower is sometimes in short supply in recovery, and much of it is already allotted to recovery-related activities. Habit can replace willpower, and it makes the whole process of self-management much easier. Habit requires a lot of expenditure of willpower in the beginning, but then becomes a "no-brainer."

How much willpower does it take to drive home from work? Your habits are ingrained and allow you to drive yourself on automatic, so that your mind can wander off to more interesting topics.

One of the great ways you can nourish your vision into reality is to foster habits that support your vision. If you exercise at exactly the same time every day, you are more likely to do it. If you hold all calls, stop all interruptions, and take ten minutes at the start of every workday to prioritize your to-do list, you will work more efficiently. If you put everyone's birthdays in your day planner on January 1, you will be more likely to remember them. All these are positive habits that Larry used to make his vision become reality.

So how does one consciously create a habit? Habits are only created by repeating conscious behavior enough times so that it almost becomes unconscious. A key tool in this process is time management.

Voltaire, in *Zadig: A Mystery of Fate,* recounted this riddle: The Grand Magi asked Zadig, "What, of all things in the world, is the longest and the shortest, the swiftest and the slowest, the most divisible and the most extended, the most neglected and the most regretted, without which nothing can be done, which devours all that is little and enlivens all that is great?"

"Time," Zadig immediately replied.

Time—from one perspective it is the only thing we have to give. We trade our time for love, livelihood, community, and solitude. Time is the only thing we have choice over. We can't control others, and sometimes we can barely control ourselves. We can't control our thoughts or our feelings. But we can, and must, choose what we do in the time we have allotted to us each day.

Who is managing your time today? Your boss and your work manage some hours of your day. Some hours your family or loved ones manage. Some hours are managed by your television set. Your bodily needs manage the sleeping and eating hours. How many hours are left for you to manage?

If you are going to bring your vision into reality, you will have to manage all twenty-four hours of each precious day. Remember Victoria, the tennis pro? Here is what she had to say about time management:

"I finally got a harsh lesson about time when my Mom died. She had me late in her life, and got divorced right after I was born. To support all of us, she went back to school and got a teaching credential.

"Her life was teaching and taking care of us. That was about it. From the time I was nine, every year in the late spring, my mom would lament that she had not planted Iceland poppies, her favorite flower. She would resolve that for sure next year she would get to it. When she was ill with cancer I bought her some potted Iceland poppies. She never got well enough to put them in the ground. They dried up in pots outside her front door as she died inside.

"That is not going to be my life. I know that I don't have

forever to accomplish all I want, to see, touch, smell, and taste all I want, to serve and to love all the people I want to. I will not waste the minutes I have left, and I will not have any dream of mine dry up in pots outside my door."

Your vision is not a noble sentiment that you should get around to some day when you have time. It is not "Iceland poppies." It is your reason for living. And to make it a reality you must take charge of the only thing you can take charge of: your time.

Time management is not hard. It only requires two things, one thing that you do and one thing that you can buy at an office supply store. That is your day planner. Everyone has his or her own quirky system of using these things. Here is a simple tried-and-true system that has worked for almost all my clients: (1) Buy a planner that has a whole page (or even two pages) for each day. It's better to get one that is preprinted with the date, rather than a blank one. Any system that requires you to write in the date will probably not end up getting used. The planners with week-at-a-glance or month-at-a-glance do not have enough room for you to do the planning you need in order to manage your time effectively. (2) (This is the hard one!) Write in it every day. The best planner in the world is worthless if it is never opened. Take ten minutes every morning to plan your day.

Julie wrote in her planner during the first ten minutes of her workday. Robert had a different way to work his system:

Robert's Story

Robert did not fit my stereotype of a garbage man. He was small, wiry, and loved classical music. He had used cocaine to plow through work and alcohol to unwind. He had the added struggle of working every day with a team of men who continued in their addiction. But he was very clear that he was no longer going to harm his family by spending money on drugs and alcohol. And he had a very unconventional dream.

"You probably don't think too highly of waste disposal, but it has been a great job for me. My whole family is in the business, and we make a lot of money. We are an up-from-nothing business, and we carved out a particular niche that has served us very well. Too well in fact: I had enough disposable income to blow fifty grand before waking up.

"So after my first year in recovery I did the vision thing, and I got real clear about what I wanted. I wanted my kids to grow up with respect and love. I wanted my marriage to work. I wanted to be able to support my church. And I wanted to go on safari to Africa before I die.

"I also got the idea that making daily commitments worked in getting me closer to my goals. But I don't have the kind of job that fits with carrying a Daytimer around. So I bought one anyway, and I keep it at home, next to my bed.

"Now every morning, I set my alarm a half hour early. I get up and read my daily meditation, say my morning prayer, and spend five or ten minutes with my planner. I figure out what things I can do today to connect with my kids, how I can show my wife that I love her, and how I can put some money today in the trip fund. We are on schedule for taking the whole family to Africa in two years."

So what do you do in those ten minutes? Managing time has to do with setting priorities. The easiest way to do this is to assign a letter to each to-do item. An A means it must and shall be done today. Don't have many of these! B means it must be done this week, but you can change the day you do it, if other circumstances interfere. C means it needs to be done sometime, and doing it this week will be great, if you can fit it in. D means you just want to remember this item, so that you can do it on another week. Using this system you can see how a D can evolve to a C, a B and even an A over time.

But setting priorities will not implement your vision. Everyday life has enough crises and dramas to fill up your to-do list with all sorts of urgent but unimportant tasks. In order to set priorities in a new way, you must make commitments to your vision.

You already set priorities. Every choice you make, you make because that activity has taken priority over any other thing you could do. When you drank, you did so because you made that the number one priority in your life. If you drove to work, that was number one. If you cheated on your spouse or partner, that was number one. If you blew off your appointment with your tax accountant and went to the movies instead, you put the movies in the number one slot. If you chose to take care of your child and put the novel you were working on in storage, you put that kid first in line.

We don't usually like that perspective. We have all kinds of stories about why we do what we do. We go to work because we have to, to make a living. We forgot the tax appointment because we are stupid. We are involved with that other person because of fate. We must sacrifice our writing to be a good parent to our children. What these stories have in common is that they place the cause of our actions outside ourselves.

This is a fine thing to do if we don't have a vision we want to bring into the world. It is comfortable to float along down "de Nile," a relaxed piece of flotsam just swept along at the whim of the current.

Vision won't let us collapse. It demands that we see the truth. And the truth is that we choose every moment of our waking life. We don't get to choose the circumstances that the universe throws at us. But we choose how to play the cards we get dealt. We can choose to fall asleep. We can choose to blame someone else for our plight. We can choose to have a drink. Or we can choose to act.

One form of choice is commitment. A commitment, as I mean it, is not a promise, an intention, or a good idea. It is a vow you make to yourself that you will keep, no matter what. Claire understood this principle:

Claire's Story

"I made one unbreakable promise to myself the last time I went into recovery. It wasn't that I would stop using, or drinking, or partying. I would have broken that promise faster than light. Nope, I promised that, if I drank or used again, that act would prove that I was one sick girl. If I relapsed, I would commit myself to a twenty-one-day, inpatient, hospital addiction-treatment unit. I had one all picked out in the hottest, dullest town I could think of. I had had enough of relapses, and this vow was the best I could do.

"I don't know how many times that stupid little promise saved my life. I would be in the middle of longing for my next binge, and this voice inside would say, 'Shit, Claire, you don't want to spend all your saved-up vacation time in a hospital. And besides, I don't have insurance, and I'll be paying off this frigging hospital bill for the next ten years. One glass of wine is just not worth it.'"

Claire has not had a drink or used a drug since she made that commitment to herself. That is the kind of power a no-kidding, no-holds-barred, do-it-or-else commitment has. Commitment means nothing will stop you. If your children were poisoned and you had to get them to a hospital to save their lives, you would. No circumstance or excuse would get in the way.

Your vision is that important. Important enough to make "it shall be done" commitments around it. You must be willing to make A-priority commitments to each of the things you hold dear to your vision. Because commitments are so powerful, it is wise not to have more than one or two going on at any one time.

Larry made these intense commitments only about accomplishing his writing objectives. He would write until two or three in the morning to make the deadline that he set for himself. He knew it was a matter of life or death, his life as a writer. Julie focused her commitments on finding a company that was doing what she wanted to do, and then succeeding in that job beyond her supervisor's expectations.

I wrote this poem about the power of commitment.

Commitment

As the archer
draws the arrow from his quiver,
he already hears
the reverberation of the shaft
as it pierces the bull's-eye.

The wedding ritual begins
years before,
as the couple walks down the road

alone together for the first time,
and they both feel a truth
which they can barely acknowledge.

Vision structures reality.
What you commit to is already accomplished.
Between intention and completion
there are no accidents,
no stories,
no alibis,
no excuses,
no dramas,
only details.

Support

You do not have to do all this alone. Remember Zog's report in chapter 7. We humans are indoctrinated to do it alone, yet we need each other intensely. To implement your vision you will need other people. And most of all you need folks who support your vision.

Having someone cheer you on as you move forward in making your dream a reality is very supportive. There are three other things that people around you can give you to specifically support implementing your vision.

1. Alignment. One of the hardest things about staying true to your trajectory is that life is constantly throwing you curveballs. Rigidity will not work. If you sacrifice everything for the sake of one goal, you end up alienating those around you. Even if you achieve it, you may feel empty and hollow.

At my commencement exercise, when I received my Ph.D. degree, I gave the valedictory:

I would like to be able to tell you how totally happy we feel completing this long and arduous course. But it would be a lie. We actually feel a lot of things.

Relief that the torture is ending.

Guilt at the incredible pain we have caused our families, as they had to sacrifice again and again so that we could claw our way up to the top of the pile, where only survivors could stand.

Shame we feel at the fact that most of the people we started out this journey with didn't make it. Not because they were less intelligent, or inferior therapists. Mostly because of luck. We had just enough of it to hang in there far past what we expected would be required of us. Their luck, support, or economic resources didn't last. We know that some of them were better than the survivors you see in front of you.

Fear that, after all you did, and all we did, it really wasn't worth all that effort.

And anger. We have been forced to sell our integrity to accommodate a critical and unforgiving dissertation committee. We have been forced to stifle our curiosity, in order to accommodate the rigid opinions of our professors, who would brook little deviance from what they knew to be the objective truth. We have been forced to embrace stress without reservation, in order to accommodate a workload of studying that eliminated the words "free time," "weekends," and "vacation" from our vocabulary.

Did all this make us better scholars and therapists? Not really. How can we do the real work of scholarship, the heartfelt reflection on the human condition and the nature of the psyche, after every original idea we have created has been ridiculed? How can we go out and counsel others to be open and vulnerable when we have had to be fanatical workaholics just to survive?

Some of us are happy. After all, we did survive. And we are proud of that. It was an initiation of fire that went on for many years. And we are here now, at its conclusion.

So welcome us, and let's drink to victory. But if you see our smiles fade at times you will know why. And believe me, if we see your smiles slip, we know why also.

A full and rich success does not carry all this baggage. You can accomplish your dream without doing so totally at others' expense. It involves forgiving yourself when you do have to put your needs above the needs of someone you love. It entails telling the hard truth to those you love. And it entails putting your goals aside at times, to be there for the other person.

When life deals you interpersonal problems, health problems, accidents, unexpected family obligations, or any one of the jokers in the deck, you move off track.

What you need in your life is someone who knows your vision and who gently reminds you about where you were heading. This must be done without judgment. It is not wrong to go off track. You will go off track often on the way to your goal.

Making it to the target is not like shooting an arrow. The more appropriate metaphor is that of the thermostat of a furnace. If you set it to 75 degrees, and the room is at 68, the furnace will go on. The room then heats up to around 77 degrees, and it turns the furnace off. The room then cools to 73 degrees and it turns the furnace on. This back and forth oscillation is similar to the twists and turns you take on the road to your goal.

Someone who is aligned with your vision can point you to the original direction, so that you can make course corrections when it is time to get back on track.

2. Acknowledgment. Bringing in a dream is hard and often thankless work. Many hours are spent doing things that no one may see or understand, yet that are critical to your success. When your projects fail, when you receive rejection letters, when everything goes sideways, there is a great temptation to give it all up.

Acknowledgment is not an affirmation of what you are doing. What you do may succeed or may fail. Many times it needs to fail before it can succeed, like falling down when learning how to ride a bike. Acknowledgment is speaking to who you are as a person. It speaks to the courage and strength and clarity it takes to be willing to fail for the sake of your goal.

You need a few folks in your life who hold you in high enough regard that they see through the details of success and failure and see your essential self, the self who is willing to keep moving forward. And sometimes they need to speak to that part of you, to remind you that it is there.

Gail, the escrow officer we met in chapter 7 told me a story about acknowledgment:

"My boss was a master at acknowledgment. I remember three weeks back from treatment, my desk was covered with a pile of stuff I still hadn't been able to climb to the top of. I was feeling crummy, depressed, and overwhelmed. Somehow he knew.

"He called me into his office, and I was sure he was going to tell me that it just wasn't going to work out with me. He said, 'Gail, I know you are inundated with paperwork, and you probably feel pretty under the weather. And I know that the recovery work you are doing right now is going to save your life. You have the backbone to take that on, and I admire the integrity it takes to come in every day and handle all that you have to handle while you are getting clean and sober. You have my respect and support all the way.' That talk pulled me through that very rough time."

3. Celebration. The celebration at the end of the road will be joined by many. What you need are a few people who are willing to celebrate the way stations, the tiny victories along the way.

Accomplishing one small step, and celebrating it, gives you a much-needed pause. With the help of someone who is willing to rejoice with you, you can look back on the path you have traveled and appreciate the distance you have come. The final destination is out of sight for a long time. But each step brings you closer. Celebrations keep hopelessness away.

Robert, the man who is going to Africa, talks about incorporating celebration into his family's life: "I've got my whole family saving for our safari. It really touches me to have my little boy put a nickel in my hand and say, 'This is for the trip, Dad.' We have a big poster in the dining room. Each time we get a thousand dollars closer to our goal, we have a big celebration dinner. I show everybody the savings book, and we all talk about what we want to see on safari."

CHAPTER ELEVEN

What about the Rest of Us?

What Is an Addiction?

Louis Armstrong said to one interviewer, "If you have to ask what jazz is, you'll never know." There is a lot of wisdom in that answer. He is implying that jazz isn't something you know by verbally defining it. You know it by hearing it, living it, being moved by it.

Whenever we try to trap this wondrous, terrible, fascinating thing called addiction into a net of words, we end up tripping over the limitations of our words. There was a debate in the early 1980s about whether we could consider treating cocaine use as addiction in treatment. In those days, some clinicians argued that every addiction needed a symptom of physiological withdrawal. Many folks kicked cocaine with no adverse physical symptoms to speak of. Was it therefore an addiction? Anyone strung out on it had no question. But the experts struggled with their definitions.

I am suggesting in this chapter that we forget trying to come up with a rational, linear, perfectly crafted definition of addiction. We do not need one that definitely diagnoses whether you are addicted or not. We will just assume that you already know the answer to that question, and that it is affirmative. One definition I particularly liked came from an old-timer who said, "An addiction is anything you have to go to a Twelve Step program for." That is a definition that comes from living with addictions, not from studying them academically. We will be entering into the land of each of several addictions. Our guides will be folks who have lived inside these prisons. They will be sharing ways they managed work during their recovery.

Addictive Eating

If a cocaine addict had to snort a tiny line every morning and then stay clean the rest of the day, there would be very few recovering cocaine addicts. That is the discipline demanded of a recovering food addict.

Let's make the hypothetical situation even more difficult. Let's say that society was always barraging the cocaine addict with advertising messages about how cocaine can make you happy. Images of a contented warm family, sitting around a holiday table freebasing crack cocaine. And let's have society paradoxically also attack the addict for looking ugly when she snorts too much. That is the world the food addict faces, as Betty can affirm.

Betty's Story

"I remember holding my little baby and gently biting her back and growling, 'I love you so much I'm going to gobble you up.' She would squeal with laughter.

"What we love, we want to devour. We want to have it all for ourselves. I loved food, and food loved me. I wanted it all, and I gained 150 pounds before I could stop myself.

"I got help from everyone; OA [Overeaters Anonymous], a sponsor, a therapist, mood stabilizers, my church, my husband, and a couple of my co-workers. Today I eat sanely. I do not want to lose weight. I do not binge or purge. I know I will never weigh 125 again, and that is just fine with me. I am proud to eat four preplanned moderate meals a day, with no snacks in between.

"Work turned out to be the biggest threat to my recovery. The doughnuts, the birthday cakes, the TGIF parties, the candy dishes—the office was a food minefield that I had to walk every day. At first I tried having 'healthy' food in my purse to eat instead, but I found out that eating anything seemed to open up the floodgates. After a few carrots, I would find myself prowling from desk to desk, looking for chocolate.

"I had to keep it simple. No food, nothing but water, from the moment I walked through the office doors until I walked out again. I told a couple of my good friends, who worked in cubicles near me, about my rule. It helps to know they are watching me to support me in my recovery. Now the office is a No Eating Zone and is finally a safe place to be."

Since drinking during office hours is no longer chic, eating has come to replace it as one way workers manage their stress. Sugar is a poor antianxiety medication, but it is omnipresent at the workplace.

Talking about food forms a mainstay topic of office conversations. What new doctor's diet I am on, what I ate last night, who is fat and who is thin—the topics are endless.

Betty stopped obsessing about her next meal and stopped trying to lose weight. Her four preplanned meals lacked the interest of bizarre food group diets, or the sacrifice of starvation, or the roller-coaster ride of weight loss and gain. Her story was boring. Sanity is not dramatic.

Along with sane eating, she taught me about another important recovery tool. When I first went into recovery, I figured that exercise would help me recover. I had been pretty much a couch potato up until that time. So I started training to run a marathon. This is the addictive mind at work. After running out my knees, I went back to watching other people exercise on TV. Betty was much wiser.

"Diet and exercise. Diet and exercise. That was the litany of my Inner Food Judge. I could binge if I worked out. I was a lazy slob. It never stopped attacking me, until I got to the point where I would eat to shut it up.

"When I crawled into sanity, I realized that all that yelling at myself about how I wasn't exercising enough was making things worse. So I started a simple movement plan; didn't even call it exercise. I didn't do it to get a hard body or to run a marathon or especially to lose weight. I did it to feel better."

Tool #1: Sane Exercise
(Worksheet 11–1)

The goal of sane exercise is just to move around for a short time each day. It is not a cardiopulmonary workout or a muscle-toning regimen. It is simply to get you breathing and in motion in a way that does not cripple you, bore you, or become a New Year's resolution you have to break. The rules are simple. Do something each day.

Betty offered to show her worksheet for her second week. You can see that this is a no-fail program. A few minutes is great!

Sane Exercise Record

Each day log how many minutes you did some
simple exercise: walking, stairclimbing, hiking, and so on

Month: _May_   Week: 1__ 2✗3__ 4__ 5__   Comments: _I did it!_

	10 min.	15 min.	20 min.	25 min.	30 min.
Monday	12				
Tuesday	5				
Wednesday		16			
Thursday	10				
Friday			22 Yea!		
Saturday		14			
Sunday	10				

Nicotine Addiction

We all know that if we smoke regularly, it will be a key element in causing our death. That doesn't seem to slow us down much. For many of us kicking cigarettes was as hard as or harder than kicking any other fiercely addictive drug. Here is my story:

David's Story

"I never thought about giving up cigarettes when I went into recovery from drinking and drugging. It was just too hard to handle the drinking. I couldn't imagine taking anything else on.

"Recovery takes a while to sink in. Two years later I was

working in a drug-free addiction treatment center. The rules were even stricter for the staff, and included no smoking. I was teaching classes in addiction and doing private therapy with folks in recovery. I was also sneaking off to smoke where no one would see me.

"I tried one last time to quit. I went cold turkey for a couple of months. Then the new, super-low-tar cigarettes came out. They tasted like breathing urban air. These were fine to smoke! I went back to my old habit, and within a month I was on Benson and Hedges menthols. I finally got it. Addictions are alike. I couldn't have one beer or one cigarette.

"I was teaching a graduate psychology class in addiction treatment at the time. I had challenged the entire class to change one habit in their lives so they could experience how difficult change really is. I announced to them that they could be my support, because I was going into recovery from cigarettes. The class lasted for three months, and every week I checked in with them. That was what I needed to get over the hump. I never took another drag."

Getting co-workers, or students, in my case, behind your recovery can be a great support, as long as you stay clean. But it can be very alienating if you relapse. All my fellow therapists at the addiction treatment center where I worked became potential threats when I sneaked away to smoke.

Environmental support is usually not enough to get you free from this addiction. Unfortunately the environment at work provides as many examples of people who could not quit as it does of people who succeed. The shift must come from within before it sticks.

In chapter 8, we talked about doing perspective work. The next tool takes perspective work to the next level. I recommend you go back and reread Tool #1 in chapter 8 to get yourself up to speed for this next tool.

Tool # 2: Out of the Box

First grab a roll of masking tape. Now I know you would rather find the easier, softer way and try to do this in your head. But this just doesn't work as well as an intellectual exercise. You need to get with your body. So go get some masking tape. Got it? Good!

Now make a human-sized tic-tac-toe board on the floor. It should look like this, and it should have room to stand comfortably in any square.

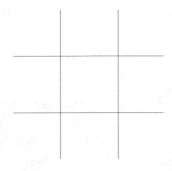

Great! Now, grab nine sheets of paper and a pen and stand in the middle square. This is your box. It is the perspective you hold that keeps you stuck. It is the core belief that blocks you from seeing a bigger picture. When we are in our addictions it often is something like "I can manage this" or "I don't care what anyone else says, I will do what I want to do!" In recovery it can be beliefs like "Anyone who uses is an addict" or "I know how you should recover" or "When I used I was bad!"

The purpose of this exercise is to move outside those beliefs and into free choice. So go ahead and choose a limiting belief about smoking, or recovering from smoking. Write it down on a sheet of paper and put it at your feet in one of the outside boxes. Imagine another perspective on the situation. Write it down, and toss it into that box. Do this seven times, until each box has a perspective about the issue in it. Throw a blank sheet into the eighth box, in case a perspective comes up you want to add. Make sure you include both positive and negative perspectives.

My grid on quitting smoking looked like this:

Smoking relaxes me.	Smoking is killing me.	I look cool when I smoke.
I am too weak to quit.	I'll quit someday.	I can smoke low tar.
Smoking is like drinking.	I should stop. It's an ugly habit.	I refuse to stop!

Next, step into each square and really try on that perspective. State it, feel it, and don't argue with it. Get into it. Feel it in your body. Then step back into the middle square.

When I stepped into "I refuse to stop!" the conversation inside went something like: "No way is anyone going to take my cigarettes away. Damn it, I have given up enough! This is my last vice, and my last stand. I am not some Goody Two-shoes, vegetarian, New Age wimp. I am a rebel—always have been and always will be. And my smoking proves it!" I felt strong, righteous, and pissed off.

When I stepped back into the middle square I could see why it had been so hard to quit. I had a vested interest in rebellion, and somehow I had equated not smoking with being weak.

Once you have stood in all the boxes, go back to the center one. Now that you have tasted the worldview inside each perspective, you are ready to choose one as the perspective you are going to take on as your new home. Step into it, and see how the other perspectives look.

When I stepped into "Smoking is like drinking" and looked at "I am too weak to quit," I realized that that would be true if I were alone. But I had learned in my recovery from alcoholism that I wasn't alone. I could use the support of others to give me the strength I lacked. That was when I got the idea of using my class as a support.

Finally, turn around and look outward, with all those perspectives at your back, and the rest of your life ahead of you. What do you see? Step away from the grid, and into the rest of your life.

Handling Smoking and Nonsmoking Co-workers

Smoking, more than any other addiction, breeds relapse. Researchers suggest that it is because we take hundreds of micro-doses whenever we smoke a pack of cigarettes. This may create a stronger habituation response than would taking one major daily dose. Relapse will continue until the denial is finally broken down enough for the smoker to acknowledge the extent and power of the addiction.

As the United States becomes more aware of the health hazards of secondhand smoke, smoking is becoming banned in more and more environments. That makes adult smokers outlaws, with all the thrill of being bad that teenage smokers have always enjoyed. This only seems to entrench the smoking behavior. To the degree that we demonize the smoker, we stop seeing their suffering and we alienate them from recovery.

No one is more righteous than a recent ex-smoker. By condemning current smokers you push them further away from ever being able to use you for support. You can't make them quit, but you can model recovery for them. To those who are still trying to quit, you can give the message that you support their recovery and you accept that they may relapse along the way. Try something like, "I know quitting smoking is rough. It took me lots of tries until I finally made it. Know that I am rooting for you, and I am not going to judge you if you slip." This is such a healing message to give out!

Debting

Of all the addictions, this one receives the least social support for recovery. One estimate I read states that on average every human being in the United States receives three applications a year for credit cards. Taxpaying adults receive at least two a month. These are invitations to debt.

Capitalism requires consumers in order to prosper. If you look at the amount of time we spend thinking about buying things, or working to earn the money to buy things you realize a curious fact. We are a culture that has placed our attention more on materialism than on any other value. Ancient Greece valued philosophy. Ancient

Rome valued conquest and entertainment. Medieval Europe valued faith. Renaissance culture valued political intrigue and innovation. Nazi Germany valued world domination and obedience. In each of these examples a significant amount of time and life energy was devoted to honoring these values.

This is not a judgment. Any value has its positive and negative elements. But in a culture in which The New Shiny Purchase is king, debting will be rewarded, and the negative consequences of addictive spending will be minimized. When you wake up from the dream state you can become frightened by the extent of your denial. Listen to Frieda:

Frieda's Story

Frieda had found out about me from my workingsober.com Web site. She was an intense, petite, dark-haired woman who came because she wanted out of her nine-to-five job. She was starting her own company from her home, and she wanted coaching and support. She would consult with me once a month face-to-face for two hours, and always paid in cash. She wasn't ready to tell me about her addictive spending until three months into our work together.

"I was paying my rent on my credit card when I finally realized what I was doing to myself. I remember the afternoon that I knew I was powerless over spending. I was lying on my couch (bought with my credit card). I was listening to my stereo (bought with my credit card). It was Jimmy Buffet, 'Wasting away in Margaritaville.' There was a stack of unpaid bills, including five credit card bills, on my new coffee table (bought with my credit card) in front of me. I listened to him sing, 'But I know, it's my own damn fault.'

And I realized that I was an addict, just like him.

"I had been trying to manage my money for years. I was in such a mess that the nonprofit debt reduction service wouldn't take me. I was paying eight hundred dollars a month in interest on credit cards, and even when I didn't charge anything, the amount I owed would increase. I was working overtime to make my bills, and it was just getting worse. I was going downhill fast. But I had a wardrobe you would die for.

"I figured out that putting a credit card in my hand was like putting a margarita in the hand of the guy Buffet was singing about. So I took out my wallet and cut them all up.

"I got a sponsor in DA [Debtors Anonymous], and worked out a budget I could live with. I call together my pressure relief group whenever I am facing making a major change in the way I spend my money. I work the Steps. I go to some open AA meetings, just to be around good recovery, even though I don't have a drinking problem. I am still in a lot of old debt, but I will never incur unsecured debt again. If I don't have the cash for it, I don't buy it. No credit cards for this cookie!"

Somehow the financial community discovered that she was an entrepreneur. It was probably her subscription to the trendy business magazine *INC*. She reports that she gets offers at least three times a week to open credit card accounts, start unsecured lines of credit, and other lending schemes to lure her back into the land of unsecured debt. About once a month she gets an actual credit card in the mail. It is as though alcohol companies got the names of the members of AA and sent them complimentary bottles of booze every week.

"I use my scissors a lot!" she told me. "But it is always hard to cut them up. There is so much that I really need right now. The hard part of my recovery was feeling like I was a loser if I couldn't buy what I wanted. The work you did with me about collapsed distinctions really cleared that one up for me."

What Frieda was referring to is a major problem most recovering people face. In the last tool, Out of the Box, we looked at a way of working with core beliefs that keep us stuck. Often the reason that a belief ends up turning into glue has to do with the way the belief is structured. When we put the dysfunctional belief under a microscope, we often discover two beliefs wound around each other. The distinction between them has collapsed. Once we tease them apart, we can choose which part we want to keep and which we want to discard.

Tool #3: Disentangling (Worksheet 11–2)

Take a belief, perspective, position, or stance that you hold and that you think is getting in your way. Write it down. Now just pretend that this belief is actually two beliefs linked together. Usually one belief is the loud belief on the surface, and the other is a hidden, more secretive position. Under each belief state what you know to be true. Tease out what you can. Remember, you can believe either one or both beliefs, but you do not have to link them together. Frieda's disentanglement looked like this:

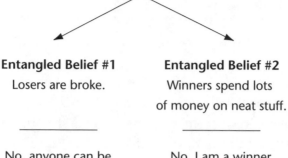

Original Belief:
If I can't buy what I want, I am a loser.

Entangled Belief #1
Losers are broke.

_____

No, anyone can be
broke at times.

Entangled Belief #2
Winners spend lots
of money on neat stuff.

_____

No, I am a winner
because I don't spend
money foolishly!

_____

Lesson: I realized that I am not what I buy, and even that not buying something makes me stronger than giving in to the urge. The belief that I was a loser was like a virus. It infected so many of my thoughts. It kept me stuck in jobs I hated. But as of today, I am weeding my inner garden.

Starting her own business and dealing with her debting issues became a substantial burden for Frieda. At times cash came flowing into her operation, and she felt the compulsion to spend it. She used the Craving Deconstructor from chapter 3 (worksheet 3–2) to manage her desires.

"I knew I was in deep trouble when I got my first check in the mail. Right away the junkie spender voice inside me said, 'Yippee! Let's go shopping!' I knew if I didn't get someone else in the loop, that I could easily blow every-thing I wanted to accomplish.

"So I set up a system to interrupt my spending impuls-es. Every cent that comes in goes into the business account, and the checks from that account require two sig-natures. No ATM card. Every week I sit down with my bookkeeper, and we agree on any purchases that need to be made. Then we both sign the checks for those pur-chases. My addict hates this procedure. Which is fine by me."

Gambling

Sam came to me as a therapy client. He was thirty-eight years old, lived by himself, and managed a wholesale plumbing supply house. He had spent his retirement account and desperately needed to tell a stranger about his secret life.

Sam's Story

"The casinos treated me like a millionaire. I would call and tell them I wanted to come up for a weekend. They would wire me first-class tickets and pick me up at the airport in a limo. It was 'Mr. H' this and 'Mr. H' that as they tucked me into my suite. They paid for my meals, my booze, everything, and I do mean everything!

"I would drop anywhere from five to twenty grand in a weekend. Sure, sometimes I came out a winner. I would always think back on those times. I would conveniently forget the many Mondays, crawling back to work broke, exhausted, and defeated. They made plenty off of me.

"You've got to understand, I am not rich. Sometimes

half of what I made went to gambling, or to paying off the debt I ran up from gambling.

"I could pull it together for a while. Betting on sports, maybe some pickup games with my friends. No big deal. And I am a pretty good player. I would usually walk away with some fun money in my pocket. Things were manageable.

"But sooner or later, the fantasies would come back. The memories of big wins. The rush of high stakes. The respect I felt. The juice. And I would have to make that telephone call.

"Walking into the casinos, you walk past the losers: eyes glazed, arms sore from loading coins and pulling handles on slot machines for days at a time. I finally got it. That is me. Only they make more per hour from me than from the zombies.

"Last week I got the hunger again. But my credit cards were maxed out and I had nothing left to spend. I started thinking, 'You know, Sam, you are good at poker. You could just take some of the store money and win a lot. Then Monday you could put back your stake and no one would know the difference.' Then something hit me—I was headed for jail. I am no crook, but here I was plotting to rip off my boss. I need some big-time help."

Gambling is as American as a cold beer, a Marlboro, a credit card, or apple pie. None of those things is necessarily addictive. Yet some people are severely addicted to them. And the advertising that these industries create exacerbates the cravings addicts feel.

Gambling is a multibillion dollar industry. Las Vegas is the fastest-growing city in the United States. Casinos are springing up throughout the country. Weekly state lotteries are common. In a world that is getting more and more caught up in gambling fever, maintaining gambling sobriety is a challenge.

But the real challenge, Sam acknowledged, was inside him, not outside. He came to see that the gambling binge was a part of a larger self-destructive cycle.

"I finally got the whole picture. It was like a wave. The top of the wave was me at the casino, living high. The crash started on the plane ride back, when I counted up my losses. By about Wednesday, the real trough of the wave started. I would call myself a jerk. I would look at all the unpaid bills.

"Usually about a week or two after the trip to Vegas I would begin to get really scared at how out of control I was. Then I would add up everything I owed, and put that number up on my refrigerator to remind me how badly I was messing up. It was like I thought that if I could hate myself enough, I could break the cycle.

"Once I started getting some money back in the bank, I would just stop seeing that piece of paper on my refrigerator that said, 'You owe $87,500 because of your gambling!' I would pay down some of my cards and pretend that I had everything under control. Soon the fantasies of being back at the tables would start, and the wave would begin building again."

Sam came to realize that he needed to focus on the troughs as well as the peaks of this wave. He saw that the fierce, angry judgments were as much a part of the addiction as the playing cards and poker chips. He found the next tool particularly helpful in working with his self-hatred.

Tool #4: Facing the Judge

In chapter 1, we sent the Inner Judge on vacation. Now it is time to call him or her back for a face-to-face encounter. Begin by using a pen or some crayons to draw the face of your Inner Judge. Do not let your Judge judge your artwork. This is just to get an image in front of you.

Next, give your Judge a name. This way you assert that the Judge is just one of many voices inside your mind. (No, this does not mean that you are crazy. They exist in your imagination. Voices are a metaphor for parts of you. Schizophrenics actually believe they are hearing the voices speaking to them.)

Now make a list of all the things that your Judge tells you. All the criticism, faultfinding, and condemnations. Use shorthand, just to get the general topic. Then go on to the next one. Keep writing until your Judge starts to run out of things to say.

Here was the beginning of Sam's list:

Judge Dread's Judgments:
- Fat
- Stuck in dead-end job
- Gambling addict
- Sex addict
- Eat and drink in binges
- In debt
- Rotten son to my mom
- Can't stay in relationships

It went on for a couple of pages. He was afraid it might go on forever. But eventually, the Judge's voice started repeating itself, and Sam could say, "Nope, Judge, I have that one down already. Come up with something else." Finally, there was nothing else to add. Sam felt great when he exhausted his Judge Dread.

The next step is to give your Inner Judge a shape. Find a sculpture, doll, or some sort of figure that captures the energy of your Judge. Keep that figure handy, and when you are tired of listening to its voice in your head, cram the statue out of your sight.

Sam's Inner Judge was named Judge Dread. He found a figurine of the cartoon character Judge Dread for his desk. My Inner Judge is named The Mouth. I have an ashtray in the form of a wide-open mouth with a long tongue hanging out. When Sam realizes that he is listening to his self-hatred and self-judgment too much, he takes Judge Dread and shoves him in a drawer or tosses him against the wall. I stuff bean bags into my Mouth ashtray to shut him up. It is quite satisfying.

Sam told his co-workers that he had a problem with gambling and that is why he would not be entering any office betting pools. He heard a lot of judgment from Judge Dread and worried that folks would draw away from him if he told the truth. Instead he got the opposite reaction: folks came up and thanked him for his honesty. Some of them were struggling with their addictions, and through his opening up, they could begin making the office a safer place for themselves.

Sex Addiction

Werner first came to me with his wife, Leeann. They had been married two years, and they needed couples counseling. She had just accidentally discovered that he had been having an affair at the office. They both wanted the marriage to survive this crisis. Werner had cut off the other relationship and was working hard to repair the rift between him and his wife. After their third visit, he asked if he could have a private session with me. In that session, the whole truth came out.

Werner's Story

"For years, I just said to myself, 'I am a highly sexual individual, and that is just who I am!' I need to have sex two to three times a day, either with a partner or masturbating, and it has been that way since I was a teenager.

"It started unwinding for me after I married Leeann. She didn't want that much sex. So I resorted to a lot of pornography, in my car or in men's rooms or after she had gone to sleep.

"But I wanted more. I had always had a number of girlfriends at the same time. They didn't know about each other, and I could go from one to the other until I had enough. But now being married had stopped all that.

"I started using prostitutes. It made me feel slimy, but I needed them. I could exhaust myself with a hooker, and then go home to Leeann and fall asleep with her. I always practiced safe sex, but I still worried about infecting my wife with some incurable disease. I was so ashamed of myself.

"It was almost better once I started my affair. It was a co-worker in my office, and she was as sex-starved as I was. We would meet at a motel every lunch, and sometimes after work. We would go at it, then shower and reenter the normal world. At least I didn't have to worry so much about AIDS, and the expense of my habit went way down.

"I hated all the secrets, but I didn't know how to stop. Now that affair is over and Leeann and I are back trying to build a life together. But I am going out of my skin with cravings. I am afraid that I will go back to hookers. I am sure she would leave me if she knew what a deceiver I am. How can I stop?"

At first Werner didn't like my answer. He realized that he and his wife were going to have to radically change their relationship to make it through recovery together. And he also realized that there would be a large chance that they might not make it. But he knew that if he fled from this crisis, he would just recreate it again. So he decided to use the six S's, a tool for couples going into recovery.

Tool #5: The Six S's

Many couples split up when one of them goes into recovery. This tool is like a road map, showing the towns the two of you have to go through as a couple to get to stable recovery.

Sharing recovery. This is the hardest location to get to, yet it is necessary to get there before you can go any further as a couple. The addict has to acknowledge that he or she is powerless over the intensity of the cravings. This was where Werner had arrived when he sat in my office and "confessed." Then the addict's partner must acknowledge that she or he is also powerless, powerless over fixing, changing, or controlling the partner. If the partner fears change or won't let go of blame, then the couple faces probable destruction.

Leeann rose to the challenge. She was stunned when she heard about Werner's secret life. She was hurt and shocked. But she also got the message I was putting out that, unless they both went into recovery, it probably wouldn't work. This was her second marriage, and the first one had broken up because of her husband's infidelity. I was clear that she was not responsible for her husband's acting out. That was his choice and his problem. But she was responsible for managing her reactions from here on out, and she could use the support of a self-help group and counseling to weather this storm.

Werner started going to SLAA (Sex and Love Addicts Anonymous) and men-only SAA (Sex Addicts Anonymous) meetings. She went to CoSA (Codependents of Sexual Addiction), and they both went together to a monthly Recovering Couples Anonymous meeting.

Storming. The first two months of recovery were very rocky! Leeann was angry at Werner for lying to her. She was also angry that she had to go to recovery groups when he had the problem. She came close to filing for divorce several times. Werner was angry also. He hated giving up his addiction. He hated the groups, where he had to let down his denial and see how destructive this pattern had been in his life. He hated being married and therefore forced to look at this mess. They would fall into blame wars that left them both hurting. Weekly couple's work focused intensely on teaching tools for fair fighting like the Ladder (worksheet 4–4), the four C's (see chapter 4), and the Rule of Three (see chapter 8).

This scenario played itself out a few times in those early months: Both partners would storm out of the house, not speaking to each other, and go off to their individual support groups. There they would let off steam and begin to see some more perspectives on the issue. After their meetings were over, they would meet back at their front door and laugh, or sigh, but go into their house together, ready to try again.

Shame. Both partners went through shameful times; Werner for all the suffering he had caused others, Leeann for choosing unavailable men. When they kept their shame to themselves, things would start to go sour between them. When they were able to share their shame with each other, there was a sense of relief, as the truth was spoken.

Sadness. Both partners had to give up something that had supported them and nurtured them. Werner had to give up discharging all his feelings through sex. Leeann had to give up the fantasy of a perfect relationship. There was real grief and loss that had to be weathered along with everything else.

Sex. Sex had to be reinvented between the two of them. The focus shifted from intensity, frequency, and variety of sexual experiences to communication, intimacy, and security. They each had to become more open as to their likes, dislikes, and fears about sex. When Werner was finally able to tell Leeann about his childhood molestation, something significant shifted in their sex life. They began to encounter each other as equals, rather than stereotypes playing out conventional roles.

Spirituality. Both because of the influence of the Twelve Step programs they were in and because of Leeann's upbringing, they decided to find a church they could feel comfortable in. This took a lot of shopping, but both of them knew it was important. When they finally found it, they invited me to their recommitment ceremony. Many folks in the church were friends of theirs from their meetings, and we all knew how hard they had worked to get to this place. In my experience, couples who hold a larger context for their relationship than sex or survival tend to stay together.

I recommend that anyone in a partnership or marriage who is going into recovery get some couples or family work early on in recovery. A professional therapist can help clear out communication blocks and get you both on the same page.

I also recommend that you shop around for a good couple's therapist. Ask the therapist if he or she is married or in a long-term partnership. Ask how many of the therapist's clients break up in the course of therapy. Ask about familiarity with recovery issues. Ask if he or she is in recovery and if so, for how long (not a requirement, by the way; all a therapist needs is some experience with the issues specific to recovery). Keep checking your intuition. You and your partner need to feel comfortable with this person or it may not be worth your time and money. Bad therapy can actually harm a couple, so trust your feelings and make sure you both agree.

CHAPTER TWELVE

The Twelve Steps for Managers and Leaders

Anthony's Story

 I first met Anthony when he sold my house. He was a charming, warm, and very competent agent. He called me three years later. "You are the only shrink I know, and I need some help with my drinking." He went into recovery, and within three years got a promotion to management. It turned out to be a booby-trapped gift.

"I got a whole new appreciation for the program when I became a manager of a real estate office. When I was a salesman, I was more or less on my own. No one was looking over my shoulder. It was sink or swim, and I swam pretty good. I was already three years in recovery. And I was making respectable money for the first time in my life.

"I couldn't resist it when they asked me to take over the office. Boy, was I ready to show them how an office should be run! Unknown to me, being a manager called up all my old addictive behavior.

"I needed to control my troops, watch over their prospecting, shepherd every escrow, and manage every crisis. My bosses loved me. My agents were ready to kill me. But the way I looked at it, I demanded excellence, and those agents were just going to have to come up to my standards. They could join me or get out of the boat!

"It wasn't really a heart attack, just angina, but it was enough to shock me awake. 'Caused by chronic stress,' the doctor told me. Well, I had way too much of that. And I was creating it! I was scared enough to go back to the program, and back to the Twelve Steps, and take another look.

"It wasn't a very pretty sight. I saw that I had become controlling and manipulating. I was acting like I was the king of the universe. I went back to Step One, and replaced 'Management' for 'Alcohol.' 'We admitted we were powerless over management and that our lives had become unmanageable.' Well, that was very close to home!

"It took me three months. I started going to CODA (Codependents Anonymous). I got a sponsor and I did the Steps again. It totally changed the way I managed my office. My agents became friends, rather than profit centers. And I guess I became a human being, too."

About the Twelve Steps

It was a stormy night in 1938, and Bill Wilson had writer's block. He had written four chapters of the book that would describe how AA worked. Now he faced writing the chapter called "How It Works" and nothing was coming. Finally, in desperation, he decided to put together an outline. When he was through with writing these ideas down, he counted them and was pleased that he had twelve. "Kind of a spiritual number," he thought to himself. These twelve ideas all sounded pretty good. He started distributing them at his meetings for comment. The Twelve Steps were crafted out of that process.

Only two hundred words. Yet the programs that were built around these words have radically altered millions of people's lives. The Twelve Steps have been rewritten to address the needs of drug addicts, sex addicts, smokers, compulsive gamblers, compulsive eaters, codependents, and even stroke recovery patients and artists.

Traditionalists and AA hard-liners insist that the Steps are effective only for alcoholics. They believe the power of the Steps gets watered down in all these other recovery programs. On the other hand, critics of self-help programs complain that the Twelve Steps lack the psychological sophistication on which to found a reliable treatment program.

Yet, every hour of every day, someone in the world is reading those words aloud to start a self-help meeting. Millions of people who seek help for their addictions and compulsions turn to the Twelve Steps for regular guidance.

The last words of the Twelve Steps suggest that we "practice these principles in all our affairs." Business affairs are the focus of this chapter. This chapter is written for people who have two life experiences. The first is that you, the reader, have some personal knowledge about the nature of the Twelve Steps. Ideally, you will have used them somewhere along the way in your own recovery. If you are not familiar with them, reading a guide to the Twelve Steps will help you better understand this chapter (*A Gentle Path through the Twelve Steps* by Patrick Carnes, published by Hazelden, is an easy place to start).

The second life experience is that you have been or are now in a position in your work where you have supervision responsibilities over others.

Working with Anthony inspired me to begin to imagine the Twelve Steps as a management program as well as a recovery program. He helped me see that the ideas of recovery applied outside the limited realms of addiction treatment. Others in the field (Melody Beattie, Jackie Schiff, Denise Breton, and Christopher Largent) are looking at society as addicted and in need of treatment. It takes a big shift in perspective to see other, deeper addictive and destructive patterns in the workplace.

The Problem

How can the perspective of the Twelve Steps help managers? You don't need a program of recovery unless there is some sort of addiction. Is work an addiction? That question brings up a whole slew of other questions: Why do so many people hate their jobs? Why do people dread Monday? Why do they pray for five o'clock to come? Why do they dislike their bosses, co-workers, and customers? Why do they live waiting for vacations and retirement? Why do some people enjoy jobs that may be quite menial, while other people hate jobs that sound ideal from the outside? Why is contentment so hard to find in the workplace? If it is not the work itself that is the problem, then what is the problem?

What makes some people love their work and others abhor it? The people who most enjoy their jobs feel that they express themselves through their work. They don't give themselves away at work, they throw themselves into work and find themselves through making their vision into reality. They are in a minority.

Others, to one degree or another, detest their work. They feel that work is a prison where they have to do time before getting released at the end of the day. One client of mine put it succinctly, "My boss is an arrogant jerk. My co-workers are out to stab me in the back. My customers just want to exploit me for every nickel they can squeeze out of me. And I'm supposed to love my work? Right!"

The verb "to addict," according to *Webster's New World Dictionary,* means, "to give (oneself) up (to a strong habit)." Many people feel they must unwillingly give themselves to their work. The economic necessity of giving over your autonomy to a work environment that feels abusive is the cause of resentment toward work.

What makes one work site seem to be an invigorating challenge and another one feel like a penal institution? People who work for a boss who respects them enjoy and take pride in their work. People who work for a boss who wants to control and demean them come to hate their work. Both bosses have authority. According to *Webster's,* authority is "the power or right to command." But the second has become *authoritarian:* "believing in or characterized by an absolute obedience to authority. An advocate or enforcer of such obedience."

The compulsion to use drugs and alcohol comes to feel like an authoritarian boss. It controls the addict. Addicts and alcoholics feel powerless in their addictions. They are unwilling victims of their compulsions. They don't feel like they have a choice. They are slaves to their addiction.

Many people at work share these feelings. They feel they have no power or influence over their bosses or over the corporations they work for. They feel as if they don't have a choice, since most jobs are equally disempowering. They have to survive, put a roof over their heads, and take care of their families. So they sell themselves into slavery every Monday morning.

They are right. Let us not blame the victims. I can hear the managers already: "They have an attitude problem! This is a great place to work, and if they don't like it they can just leave!" That perspective itself smacks of authoritarianism. Rather than hearing the problem, the manager tries to eliminate the messenger.

The truth of the matter is that managers feel even more pressured than those they manage. They fear rebellion in the ranks, insubordination, laziness, theft, or incompetence from those they supervise. And they fear criticism or termination from those above them.

Work is not safe. It is not nurturing. Often it is merciless. When profits take a dive, programs for "participatory management," "flexible scheduling," "family-centered work shifts," "two-way communication," and "team-building" go right out the window. In crisis, the default management style is usually harsh authoritarianism.

Look at the language of modern business: "hostile takeovers," "poison pill," "white knight." The words themselves express the kill-or-be-killed mentality that underlies the consciousness of contemporary capitalism.

For anyone who has gone through his or her own recovery, this description of the psychic landscape of business will look quite familiar. The paranoia, the aggression, the need to protect, the illusion of power, and the dread of hopelessness are all integral parts of the world of an actively using addict/alcoholic.

The negative obsession of the workplace is the misuse of power through the authoritarian control of others. People misuse authority out of egotism, out of arrogance, and out of fear. The business community is so thoroughly indoctrinated into a worldview of scarcity, danger, fear, power, and control that it doesn't even recognize its behavior is obsessive. Abuse seems normal.

This situation looks every bit as hopeless as any addiction. It is time to turn to the Twelve Steps.

Step by Step

Step One. We admitted we were powerless over the misuse of power and control, and that our lives had become unmanageable.

Step One confronts us with the question: What is the nature and what are the limitations of our power? What is under our control and what isn't? As recovering people, we discovered (when we did not participate in addictive behavior) that we had some limited power in our lives. When we used, we lost the ability to predict what would happen.

We also discovered that no self-improvement book in the world seemed to make a dent in our addictive behavior. We envied those who just woke up one day and stopped drinking or drugging or bingeing. But when we tried on the myth of autonomy it backfired. "I can do it myself" soon turned into "I'm sorry. It will never happen again. I promise!" It was only in treatment centers, in communities of worship, and especially in anonymous meetings that we found the social and spiritual support we needed to surrender control and get back our lives.

In recovery, we learn to put down the cup of false power and pick up a cup of humility mixed with gratitude. At work, it appears that we do not have that option. Everyone is looking to you to take charge and stay in control. The last thing they want is surrender. This is an unmanageable situation, if ever there was one. Step One simply asks us to acknowledge that fact.

Step Two. Came to believe that a Power greater than ourselves could restore us to sanity.

I once knew a sales manager who was so afraid of his agents that he would drive past the parking lot, checking to see who was in the office. If the car of a problem agent was parked there, he would drive home for the day. Later in his career, he became an autocratic leader who so frightened his subordinates that no one dared to be truthful with him. He would tell the parking lot story as a joke about how scared he was starting out. He stopped being scared and began making others afraid. Insanity is alive and well in all levels of management.

People admire power. They want you to order them around so they can resist, complain, rebel, comply, or call in sick. The manager gets forced to play Good Daddy/Mommy or Bad Daddy/Mommy. And no one grows up.

A voice in our mind shouts, "It is foolishness to imagine we can really change the workplace. No way could we have work be a place where people acted out of gratitude rather than servitude. Not at my job." Yet it is just as foolish to imagine that a bunch of drunks could get together and get sober when the finest professionals in the world couldn't get them to stop drinking and using. Perhaps the same Power that restored you to sanity could do a job on your worksite.

Step Three. Made a decision to turn our will and our lives over to the care of God *as we understood God.*

What is God? Quite a few people have addressed that question! But recovering people have a leg up in the conversation. Theology aside, we have some firsthand experience. We don't have to wonder whether or not God exists. God is evident in the reality that we are sober today. The nouns we attach to that miracle (Jesus, Allah, Truth, Reason, Universal Will, the Fellowship, or whatever) don't really make as much difference as the reality that, without God, we weren't going to make it clean and sober. With God we do.

We learned some things about God in recovery. Things like the belief that God has something to do with love, thankfulness, amazing coincidences, patience, gentleness, self-honesty, and connection with others.

Business worships its own deities: Control, Power, Image Management, and Obsession with Profit. Ignore these entities at your peril. Most of your co-workers serve this pantheon obsessively, from dawn until they escape at night, exhausted and drained.

Control: We use authoritarianism to maintain control over those we supervise. Power: We dehumanize others and close our hearts to them, so that we can wield power over them. Image Management: We commit personal psychological plastic surgery to keep on that calm mask regardless of the fear, confusion, rage, or boredom we feel inside. Obsession with Profit: We recklessly sacrifice and squander the only commodity we really possess, our time, so that at year end the company can show a profit on the books.

Control, Power, Image Management, and Obsession with Profit: these abstract concepts devour people's lives, and we go to the slaughter, willingly serving this pantheon until the heart attack hits.

In your recovery, you must come to terms with these powerful, hungry forces. You cannot simply surrender your life to them. You have been down that road already. You serve another master now. One you know quite personally, and one who saved your life.

You cannot do it alone. You cannot single-handedly resist the tremendous pressure to conform to the demands of Control, Power, Image Management, and Obsession with Profit. Don't worry. You are not alone. Step Three reminds you to turn the whole problem over to the care and will of the force that has already transformed your life.

Step Four. Made a searching and fearless moral inventory of ourselves.

Now it is time for a new inventory, a Management Fourth Step (see worksheet 12–1). This one is about work, and more precisely about you as a manager. Remember, the Fourth Step is written down. It's easy to read a chapter in a book. It's very hard to take the time to see your own addictive controlling patterns. Recovery only comes from some hard work. So give yourself a day off. Take a personal leave day. Pull out a pen and some paper and get honest with yourself. Here are some suggested questions to begin your inquiry:

Fourth Step for Managers
Questions about Power and Control
1. Under what conditions do I demand obedience?
2. How am I feeling about the people I supervise in those moments when I demand obedience from them?
3. Who demanded obedience from me when I was a child, and how did that affect me?
4. Who demands my obedience now, and how does that make me feel?
5. What makes me feel out of control at work, and what do I do about it?
6. Examine your relationship with each person you supervise. One by one, look at the way you have used or abused power and control in your relationship with that person.

Questions about Image Management
1. What characteristics, talents, behaviors, and attitudes do I want my co-workers and supervisors to admire in me?
2. What do I need to hide about myself in order to win their admiration?
3. What else am I afraid to show others about myself?

4. What aspects of those people I supervise repel me?

5. What do I do to make sure they don't show their truth to me?

6. How much of my time and life energy do I spend presenting a false mask at work? How often am I genuine, authentic, open, and honest about my truth?

Questions about Obsession with Profit

1. What is my most truthful definition of profit?

2. What do I sacrifice in my life (for example, time, relationships, energy, rest, quality of life) in order to increase my company's profit?

3. What do I expect those people I supervise to sacrifice in order to make the company more profitable and to protect my job?

4. Open your daily planner. Divide last week into half-hour time slots, so that you have 48 time slots a day, 336 slots for the week. Count how many of these 336 slots you spent participating in each of the following activities:

Profit-related: work and work-related activities:

Not for profit: intimate relationship:

                  parenting:

                  other home/family-related activities:

                  friends:

                  community activities:

                  church-related activities:

                  recovery-related activities:

                  sleep:

                  eating:

                  health-related activities:

                  active recreation (hiking, tennis, and so on):

                  passive recreation (TV, computer):

                  other:

What do you notice about your choices?

Step Five. Admitted to God, to ourselves, and to another human being the exact nature of our wrongs.

There is no getting around this step. No one likes it. Everyone comes up with elegant excuses about why it isn't necessary. But there is a specific technology to the Twelve Steps, and Step Five is an essential element in successful recovery. The shame, denial, and guilt can only be lifted through confession. The strength to continually align ourselves with our higher principles comes from doing difficult things, like Step Five.

One piece of advice. Pick someone outside your work setting and outside your career. There is a burden placed on the person who hears your Management Fourth Step. It is not fair to them to have to transact business with you after hearing your discoveries. This is especially true of those you supervise!

It is not uncommon to have the person you share these insights with think that you are crazy. Unless they have some experience in recovery, they probably think the royal road to success is paved with Power, Control, Image Management, and Obsession with Profit. You may feel a little like Bill Wilson, wandering through the Midwest, looking for someone who understands what it means to compulsively need a drink.

Take heart. You are not alone. Share this book with a friend in recovery. Then share your Management Fourth Step with him or her.

Step Six. Were entirely ready to have God remove all these defects of character.

Business is full of self-improvement programs. There are best-selling books, tapes to listen to on your commute, videos on "achieving your personal power," motivational speakers, charismatic trainers, an entire industry devoted to helping you fix your defects of character. Each one promises to increase your power, sharpen your control, polish up your image, and increase your profits. They valiantly attempt to convince you that you can do it all yourself, with just a little help from the experts. These programs often fail to make any long-term difference.

If they did work, people would stop buying the next tape or going to the next weekend seminar. They would just get better. People don't seem to be getting happier, more productive, or more at peace. They just seem to keep buying the next packaged promise of success.

Recovery is not a self-improvement program. The last thing we need is a new and improved self. It was self-will run riot that got us into our addictions in the first place. Recovery was created by desperate men and women who finally humbly admitted that they needed the support of others to do what they could not do alone.

In business, dependency is condemned. There is something wrong with you if you don't bounce back in a couple of weeks from losing a mate, a parent, or a child. At work we see need and emotional vulnerability as a sign of weakness. "Pull yourself up by your own bootstraps" is the rule, much more than "Lean on me."

Step Six reminds us that we cannot remove our defects of character by sheer willpower. We cannot do it alone. Our transformation and personal salvation is not something we can force, or even control. There is a much larger pattern that will have its way with us.

Step Seven. Humbly asked God to remove our shortcomings.

Humility is a rare commodity in today's corporate culture. The "I can do it" style of leadership is grounded in the myth of autonomy. From that perspective, there is no problem so large that one great leader can't grapple with it and defeat it. When you succeed, you are canonized and promoted. When you fail or, even worse, when you don't even try, you are ostracized from the herd. There is always someone ready to take your place.

There is no room for losers on the corporate ladder. So how are we to deal with our defects of character? The one thing we have learned about these faults is that they don't just quietly disappear with the application of willpower. They are cunning, baffling, and powerful. And some of these defects of character can include the unjust use of power at someone else's expense, overcontrolling other people's lives out of our own fear, lying, manipulating, and placing the pursuit of profit over any other value.

One of the board games my daughter and I used to play when she was a child was called Lie, Cheat, and Steal. The only way to win was to act in a completely amoral, anti-social manner. When I read articles about corporate raiders, junk bond swindlers, corporate polluters, corrupt politicians, and armament manufacturers, I realize that others take that game seriously.

But the problem lies closer at hand. As Shakespeare said, "The fault, dear Brutus, is not in our stars, but in ourselves, that we are underlings." It is not just other people's "sociopathy" but our own "underling" human nature that is operating. We are imperfect, fallible, insensitive, and egocentric. We create much of the suffering around us.

Humility comes from surrendering to something greater than your ego. Humility cannot be forced or accomplished through an act of will. It comes from giving up.

It comes from recognizing that anything you do to correct some problems will likely only make them worse. It comes from allowing a force greater than your limited perspective to use you in promoting health and healing. Surrendering control over a situation is a very courageous thing to do. You have to let go of fixing things. Instead, you ask for guidance and trust enough to know that the guidance will come. Often it comes from other people.

There is a joke about that:

Two bush pilots were drinking together in a bar up in Alaska. One turned to the other and said, "I know there is no God!" "Oh, how do you know for sure?" asked the other pilot.

"Well," began the first pilot, "I was flying in a blizzard and my plane began falling apart. I managed to get her down barely, but the radio was out. I got colder and colder, and I knew I would soon freeze. So I prayed to God for the first time in my life. I said 'God, if you exist, save my life!'"

There was a long, silent pause between the two pilots. The second pilot couldn't contain himself any longer and burst out, "Wait a minute! That story proves God exists. You are here today!"

"Nah," complained the first pilot, "God didn't save me, some Eskimos came along to do that!"

Often we need "Eskimos" to give us guidance we are too stubborn to give to ourselves. Friends, enemies, co-workers, clients, and competitors can all serve that function.

Step Eight. Made a list of all persons we had harmed, and became willing to make amends to them all.

Step Nine. Made direct amends to such people wherever possible, except when to do so would injure them or others.

Humility is a muscle that is strengthened through use. Steps Eight and Nine are the moral, spiritual, and ethical workout we do to strengthen this muscle. Amends are the tools we use to do this work.

The most powerful lesson we can learn from making amends is that real change comes from "who we be" rather than from "what we do." Amends are a "being," not just a doing. They are not merely token apologies. To really make amends means that you forever alter the way you regard that other person. This new perspective governs the way you treat him or her in the future.

Unskillful or superficial amends can actually create more suffering. This can become a performance for the recovering person. You can lose awareness of the impact you are making on the person you wanted to make amends to. You can be doing it all for you, at their expense. You are acting once again in an abusive manner.

Even worse is the amends that may have gone over great in the moment but that was insincere at its core. An example will serve to illustrate this: In carnivals and midways there is a member of the crew whose job it is to "cool the mark." Let's call him Joe. Joe circulates through the midway with a stuffed animal under one arm. He is on the lookout for any member of the public (the "mark") who is starting to get angry because he or she is being taken by a carnival barker at a booth.

When Joe spots the angry mark, he steps up right next to the person and starts losing a lot of money fast. Then he laughs as if he is having a great time and sympathizes with the mark. The mark ends up feeling foolish. After all, he or she is mad at losing fifty dollars when Joe here just dropped a hundred and thinks it's funny. The mark wanders off, completely conned into stuffing the anger.

Workers have met Joe lots of times. "Joe" can be the new team-building consultant, the communications expert, the suggestion box, the unexpected bonus on your birthday (which happened to fall just before the strike vote). When management uses any of these techniques to defuse the anger of employees rather than to honestly improve working conditions, they become "Joe."

Amends can make you into "Joe." You might sit down and share with one of your employees the exact nature of the way you have unskillfully controlled, manipulated, and power-tripped him or her. They forgive you and tell you how impressed they are with your honesty. They begin to hope things might start getting better around here. Then you go out and do it again to them next week. They now see you as just another "Joe."

At work, amends are best made by changing your behavior. If you have done a thorough Fourth Step, you have the raw material for making a good Eighth and Ninth Step. One tool that might help is to make a list. Include each person under your leadership who showed up in your Fourth Step. Then look at how your defects of character affected that relationship. Finally, come up with a word or phrase that would serve your recovery in relationship to that person. It could look like this:

> Cheryl: Take time to really listen to her.
> Arnold: Honestly and compassionately let him
>   know that he isn't cut out for this work.
> Frank: Give him clearer instructions.
> Louise: Acknowledge her contributions.
> Mary: Patience.

Read this list daily. Revise it. Use it, instead of reacting in the old authoritarian or codependent behavior.

Step Ten. Continued to take personal inventory, and when we were wrong promptly admitted it.

Without this Step, AA would just be another good idea. There are a lot of good ideas, powerful experiences, mind-expanding forms of knowledge, and awe-inspiring adventures. They are moments in our life. But without a framework around them, moments do not coalesce into permanent structures. Many people like to collect intense moments without going through any deep structural change or development. They just go from moment to moment, with all their character defects firmly in place. Step Ten implants the learning from the previous nine Steps firmly into our lives. It shifts the focus from insight to daily application, sometimes hourly.

Recovery has failed unless we substantially transform our lives. Recovery is not really about stopping addictive behavior for a while. It is about so realigning our lives that there is no longer room for the addiction to fit into the richness of who we have become.

Recovery is the hardest and most rewarding work there is. No part of us is left untouched by its effect. The ultimate goal is not that we come out like "program robots" all spouting the same platitudes and worldview. The true goal is that we burst into bloom, each of us unique, radiant, and completely authentic. Doing our recovery in every minute of our lives grants us that miracle.

Step Eleven. Sought, through prayer and meditation, to improve our conscious contact with God as we understood God, praying only for the knowledge of God's will for us and the power to carry that out.

Step Eleven comes full circle in looking at the issue of power and powerlessness. Before recovery, we thought that we could control everything important. Our recovery began the moment we discovered that there were behaviors over which our individual will had no control. As we progressed through the Steps, we learned how to turn more and more of our lives over to the guidance and protection of something we called God.

Some of us experienced it as a voice of wisdom coming from deep within. Others felt it as guidance coming from above. The theology was not as important as was our consistency in learning to listen to this new voice in our lives and "turning our will and our lives over to the care of God as we understood God."

Step Eleven also presents us with a method for cementing this new relationship in our lives. Prayer and meditation enhance the connection with this source of guidance.

It is interesting that we don't usually think of praying for those at work. We pray for our loved ones, for those of our faith, and perhaps for peace on Earth. But our boss or the crew down on the loading dock don't usually make it into our devotions. As Zog noticed, people at work are kept at a distance. They are not to be completely trusted. They may plot to capture your job away from you. They may be forced to fire you. In a world whose foundation is grounded in cutthroat competitiveness, your co-worker may pose a greater threat than your competitors.

As long as you share these beliefs, you help cocreate a world where no one can relax his or her guard for long. What a different impact you make when you come to hold those above and below you on the corporate ladder in kindness, compassion, understanding, and love. What would happen if you also opened your heart to your customers and your competitors? With that attitude, who could predict what transformations might occur?

Anthony told me how he put this Step into practice: "Every morning, as part of my morning meditation, I bring up the face of each one of my agents. I hold them in my heart for a moment, and pray for them. Then I pray for me, that I will treat this person with humanity and brotherhood."

Step Twelve. Having had a spiritual awakening as the result of these Steps, we tried to carry this message to others who misuse power and control, and to practice these principles in all our affairs.

"A spiritual awakening"—what a radical concept. It suggests that the problem with us before wasn't our inherent evils or our sinful ways. The problem was merely that we were asleep. All our addictions and all our lack of skill came from that source, our insufficient awareness of our true nature. As we awaken, we lose the desire to go back to that comatose state. And as we awaken we see more clearly the affliction that kept us asleep.

How can we bring this perspective to others who are more asleep than we are? Well, some of us have tried grabbing their shoulders and shaking them awake. It hasn't worked too well. It is also an approach that lacks humility. Proselytizing, lecturing, and other forms of pointing out the inadequacies and deficiencies of others do not serve our recovery.

The solution is simply to live it, "in all your affairs." Find the times when your heart closes, and work toward opening it (yes, even with your boss or with your rival). Remember the phrase "attraction, not promotion"? If you are an example, people will begin to want what you have, and one by one they will come to you.

When you act from your moral guidance, at first you may find yourself temporarily alone. You may be advocating a position that takes into account the lives of people, not just the bottom line. That stance may shock your peers. If you stay true to your beliefs, you will begin to notice something very interesting. People begin to see you as a leader, and they begin taking risks like that also. Pretty soon you are definitely not alone.

I will let Anthony end this chapter with his tale.

"I remember the first managers' meeting where I spoke up and told the company president that I thought his plan to reduce the agents' commissions was not the right way to go. You definitely could have heard a pin drop. Some of my fellow managers were checking out how close the nearest exits were.

"I got blasted, all right. He told me how little I knew about the direction the real estate industry was going, and how my view was out of step with current realities. I respectfully responded that I believed we could buck the trend of our competitors to reduce agent commissions, and win some real loyalty and respect from our agents. I lost that round, but I won his respect. He saw I wasn't a 'yes man' and later on down the road I started winning some.

"Even better, a handful of my compatriots started joining me in those 'discussions' with the boss. This really helped him see that unless we took the needs of our agents into account, we were going to cut ourselves off from our source of revenue. It made me feel great to know I was willing to take personal risks for my agents' sake. It was a long way from my old 'Obey me or get out of the boat' style of management."

Leading Sober

Barbara is a fellow life coach and a friend of mine. She is a tall, attractive woman in her midfifties who gave up her life as a vice president of a large stock brokerage house to pursue her coaching career. She gave me a lot of the ideas for this chapter, so I will let her introduce it.

Barbara's Story

"My mom was a lush, in and out of recovery until she died. I saw the inside of plenty of Twelve Step meetings, both as her companion, and later as a recovering codependent. I had this bad habit of choosing men who needed mothering.

"I made it in the corporate world. I broke the glass ceiling, and might have made it to the boardroom. But the whole enterprise started to seem empty and meaningless. It was all about profit, and being Number One, and getting bonuses.

"It all started unraveling for me when one of my co-workers shot himself. I knew Louis pretty well, well enough to know that his wife had left him and he was on antidepressants. Every one else in the office just wrote his suicide off to that.

"But he did it in his office, and some of us got a chance to read his note. He wrote something like: 'I am sorry I am messing up the office. I hope it is not too hard to clean up. I just can't keep up the pace any more. I screwed up the Washburn account, and I just don't care. Tell Jenny [his wife] I am sorry for wasting her time.' I couldn't get the note out of my mind.

"This odd question began haunting me, 'For what am I working so hard?' I could look at my apartment, and my closet, and my retirement account, and the slides I have taken from all over the world. So what? I would never kill myself, but I was starting not to care. I finally knew I had to leave.

"In a sense, I copped out by dropping out of corporate life and becoming a coach. Don't get me wrong, I love my work, and my much more relaxed lifestyle. I wouldn't go back to Wall Street for any money. But I never had any lasting impact on my firm. I came and went, and they are doing business as usual. And it is so sad, because now I know it could be so much better for them."

Perspectives on Work

Barbara and I have been talking about how to make work even more relevant to people's lives. For some people that is unnecessary. They like work. Some of them get enough meaning just knowing their toil feeds, clothes, and shelters their loved ones. Or they love the rough-and-tumble excitement and stress of their job. Some like their co-workers and therefore don't mind the work so much. Others feel they make other people's lives better. A number of folks like the power, prestige, or respect they get at work.

And finally, some just enjoy doing a hard job well.

But there are many others who feel trapped, used, angry, resentful, or resigned. One study found that 83 percent of American workers are dissatisfied with their jobs. When we realize that a large majority of our waking hours are spent either at work or in some way thinking and feeling about work-related issues, we can see what a great waste of human potential it is to have the workplace something to dread.

Let's look at some of our positive and negative perspectives on work:

Work makes the world a better place: By working we provide services and products that improve the quality of life for many more people than we could touch directly. In a free marketplace they show their appreciation by paying us, and everyone who provides or receives value prospers.

Work is exploitation: Work is inherently exploitation, and recent attempts to make it touchy-feely only disguise the reality that the rich are getting richer at the expense of the quality of life of everyone below them.

Work deepens the soul: I have had conversations with transpersonally oriented business consultants who see work as an ashram in which we can discover things about our true nature and wear off the rough edges of the ego through service and compassion.

Work is a place where you can grow up: Freud, and many therapists since, assert that work and love are the two most central arenas of adult experience. It is there where we can continually mature, or where we can stagnate.

Work just is: I can't forget what Robert, the man who ran his own refuse disposal company, said to me: "I get sick of hearing about what work is supposed to do for you. Work is work. Show up, suit up, and get to it. Intellectual whining about what it should or shouldn't be doesn't put food on the table. Work is there to be done. That's it."

Work is fun: Work is exciting, challenging, and always pushing us to exceed yesterday's accomplishments. It is the best game in town.

Work is a burden: Work is what I have to do to pay for the fun I have on weekends and vacations. Besides, I am saving for my retirement, when I won't have to work anymore.

Which of these perspectives is closest to the one you hold about work? Stop reading for a moment and think about how you regard work. What is your truth about it?

Recovery forces us to question our perspective on work. "For the sake of what did you recover?" I believe that we were called to recovery. Eight out of ten addicts/alcoholics don't even get in the door to treatment and recovery. We got through the door, and every day we reaffirm our desire to live. We are a select group, with big work to do in the world, work that needs us to be clean and sober.

Applying the Values of Recovery to Work

Every one of us must discover what is our unique life project. Yours probably has something to do with making the world a more alive, nurturing, beautiful and meaningful place. I also believe that, "having had a spiritual awakening as a result of these Steps" and as a result of our recovery, we naturally want to empower others and give them the gifts of life that we have come to cherish.

Which, by extension, means that we will want to make work more alive, nurturing, beautiful, and meaningful. And we will have to create workplaces that empower everyone in them and honor the gifts that life hands us.

How can we, as recovering people, make a difference in the world of work? Anthony, in chapter 12, explored how we can use recovery to manage and lead with more compassion and humility. Knowing that, what kind of work world will we create around us? What would the workplace look like if it incorporated values like personal inventory, amends, humility, service, surrender, Higher Power, turning it over, prayer and meditation, fellowship, and spiritual awakening?

I can hear from you a chorus of "Yeah, right! I don't think so! Not where I work!" But what if we were to translate this Twelve Step language into a more acceptable dialect? It could look something like this imaginary company's values statement:

> Our company values each employee, taking responsibility for the impact of your behavior on your coworkers, and communicating skillfully with them to ensure that you have a solid working relationship with everyone on your team (personal inventory and amends).
>
> Our company values cooperation rather than an attitude of cutthroat competitiveness. We recognize that the way to succeed in the modern economy is to provide the highest level of service to our clients, customers, vendors, and even competitors. We win more lifelong clients by referring our clients to our competitors, if they can do something we cannot, than by lying to our clients in a desperate attempt to

capture all their business. The goal is quality, not victory (humility and service).

Our company values positive influence rather than rigid control. Our goal is not to manipulate, dominate, or regulate our customers or our co-workers. By creating a product of superior quality and a workplace of exciting aliveness grounded in mutual respect, we become irresistible for both our co-workers and our clients (surrender).

Our company welcomes the knowledge that the outcome of our efforts may be very different from what we expected. By staying flexible and innovative we are able to turn every challenge into an opportunity and accept every problem as an invitation to grow and change (turning it over, Higher Power).

Our company values creative, "out of the box" problem solving. We ask our co-workers to use their intuition, creativity, and the genius that each one of us possesses to solve problems and accomplish our goals. We know that people learn and think in a variety of ways, and we welcome that diversity. We encourage our co-workers to develop their connection to their inner guidance, in whatever way that comes forth for them. We create an environment where new ideas and unpopular opinions can be shared and mined for the value they contain (prayer and meditation).

We grow because of the depth to which we welcome diversity in all its aspects; age, sexual orientation, race, culture, socioeconomic status, life experience, religion, life philosophy, values, perspectives, and perceptions. We feel we have been brought together to do work together and to grow from association with each other (fellowship).

The translation is not perfect, but you can get a flavor of the essence of each principle, as it moves into the corporate world.

Creating a values-driven company may seem quite a challenge. Oh, sure, many annual reports claim that the company is "values-centered." But most of the time that is PR posturing rather than actual practice. Most companies in the United States are profit-driven, profit-centered, and profit-oriented. They are for sale to the highest bidder, and their values are as transitory as their ownership.

But occasionally I have run across a company run by people who are not willing to sacrifice their moral beliefs for a stock killing. These companies are not for sale. They are often found leading the pack in their line of work. They have phenomenally high retention rates among their employees and managers. I assert that they are in the vanguard of the next economic species to evolve from capitalism. What follows is an example of one of those corporations.

Case Study: Marriott Hotels

In 1927, J. W. Marriott Sr. started his career operating a nine-seat root beer stand in Washington, D.C. He went on to run several restaurant chains and moved from food service to lodging. His son took over the reins in 1972 and concentrated the focus of the corporation on the hotel and lodging components.

Marriott Lodging operates or franchises more than 1,800 hotels worldwide. In 1998 the annual sales of its parent company, Marriott International, Inc., exceeded eight billion dollars.

For eight years in a row Marriott has made it to the "Top 100 Companies for Working Mothers" list in the magazine *Working Mothers. Fortune* has placed it in the "Top 100 Best

Companies to Work For" list, the "Top 50 Best Companies for Asians, Blacks, and Hispanics," and their new "Most Admired Companies in America" list.

"This company places a huge value on the personal growth of its employees!" Don Semmler is senior vice president of the southeast region. When he was an area general manager in northern California, he sent the entire managerial staff of one hotel through a training program to learn coaching skills. I'll let him tell the story:

> "Take care of your people and they will take care of your customers" was the legacy that J. W. Marriott Sr. left us. The Marriott family values have given our company a super strong foundation. These values are lived on every level of this organization. Bill Marriott visits his hotels all the time, working to make them better.
>
> We all are 'tude maniacs, positive, upbeat, outgoing, honest, and hardworking. Our attitude is "Success is never final," which translates into a pride in our organization and a mission throughout the whole Marriott family of services to keep making it better.
>
> It is so exciting to work with these people. Excitement is contagious. One study of our management found that we have three times the retention rate of our nearest competitor. That is because we enjoy making ours the best hotels in the world.
>
> Let me tell you one example of how "taking care of our people" worked. I was responsible for coordinating the training in our Santa Clara Hotel. We always have a hefty training budget, and folks could spend their allotment on a variety of different offerings. But I saw a need for all of us to join together in one coordinated project and bring the whole

facility to a deeper level of connection, intimacy, and alignment.

So we created a special coaching/training experience for the facility. Thirty managers from all levels, including two hourly supervisors, came together in this highly experiential training. They went through four weekend classes, six to eight weeks apart. They were learning how to listen, how to share intimately, and how to begin to see their impact on others: in short, how to be a coach in every aspect of life. Between classes they had group telephone sessions and individual coaching, and they coached each other.

The first classes were about getting real with each other, putting down the masks we wear. People were questioning, "Jeez, what is going on here?"

But then people began to click and see their own stuff, and began to get out of their own way. It was wondrous to see people finally get it. Their faces would light up when they could see and own some pattern that had them stuck until that moment. They would get really excited about their potential getting freed up.

They took this excitement back into the workplace, and it brought all kinds of new energy to their work. How do you measure something like that? We already had employee satisfaction rate in the nineties. So anything that can give us a few percentage points higher is worth its weight in gold. That year our hotel ended up with the highest scores in the country.

The hotel industry right now is going through all kinds of consolidations, financial turmoil, buyouts. Most of the major chains are controlled by financial people with a "profit-first" orientation.

Not us. The same family that started us runs us. We simply want to be the best hotel company in the world. And to do that we take better care of the people who work for our company than anyone else does for their employees. I am proud to work here.

Building from Within

Many of us do not work for inspiring companies like Marriott. How do we change the company we are in? Some folks feel it can only come from the top. They say that, unless the CEO and the board are behind organizational transformation, it is doomed.

The next case study flies in the face of that contention.

Case Study: Corporate Environment Division, BC Hydro

BC Hydro is a large energy supply company that serves the province of British Columbia in Canada. It has six thousand employees. It is the third largest electric utility company in Canada and made more than one billion dollars last year.

Three years ago the Division of Safety and Environment faced corporate downsizing. The manager, David Balser, describes the situation facing managers in positions like his this way: "When you are staring corporate oblivion in the face, you can either cover all your bases and try to play it safe or you can say, 'Here is what we determine it means to be a great division,' devote yourself to that task, and let the chips fall where they may."

His employees began spending a significant amount of time looking at how to improve their workplace. Weathering a corporate restructuring, Balser and his group of employees became the Corporate Environment Division. Their task within the organization was to analyze the impact BC Hydro's operation had on the environment. They were to research the company's compliance with environmental issues (such as greenhouse gas emissions, endangered species, or alternative sources of energy), serve as a conduit to public consumer and environmental groups, and communicate company policy on environmental issues to the public.

Within the division, Balser and his twenty-five employees were already in the process of creating a new work environment, the people-centered workplace. Brenda Dahlie, one of the key players in this project, described it this way:

> None of us had a human resource background. Peter Lee had a background in organizational development and learning organizations. But there was no road map. We just went stumbling and glumping along. There were no rules, so we made them up.
>
> People support what they create. It is not as though this came in from the outside. We have created the people-centered workplace from the ground up, and are continuing to create it and involve everyone in this work. We always ask if we have a learning organization orientation, and then look at what is working and what isn't.
>
> It is not like we are ever going to achieve some perfected state. The opportunity to try things out and fail is absolutely necessary to make this thing work.

They all took on a mission to "create a workplace where people are supported to do and be their best." This involved creating a group that monitored the quality of the workplace as a learning organization, the community building center team. Membership rotates in four-month shifts and also involves being a part of a team learning lab, in which team members focus on systems thinking, authentic communications, and creating a shared vision.

In the monthly divisionwide staff meeting the focus is as much on relationship building and group facilitation skill building as it is on problem solving. The guiding principles for that meeting were adapted from Angeles Arrien's book, *The Four-Fold Way* (HarperSanFrancisco, 1993):

1. Show up (be fully present).
2. Pay attention to what has heart and meaning.
3. Tell the truth without blame or judgment.
4. Be open to outcomes, not attached to outcomes.

Dahlie describes how powerfully the opportunity to facilitate these meetings affects some employees: "People take on challenges and push their own barriers. They may have a fear of speaking in front of large groups. They will practice in small group settings, and end up speaking before the whole division. People are proud that they have come to see themselves as leaders, able to set their own boundaries, and show up and innovate in very creative ways."

Coaching skills are taught and used throughout the division. Often in corporate settings coaching is brought in to help the individual accomplish the goals that the corporate structure has imposed on her or his job position. Someone else, not the client and the coach, determines much of the agenda of the coaching. Balser has a strong reaction to that approach:

> We explicitly rejected that approach. My philosophy for doing that is "if you want the whole employee to come to work, you've got to coach the whole employee." If their hang-up is not knowing how to say "no," then that is what you've got to start with.

That may or may not be helpful to the items on their job description, but ultimately I don't think you can parcel it off.

You can't say, "No, we are only interested in those aspects of you as an employee that directly return value to us." This is shortsighted and narrow-minded. If you want to engage the whole person, engage their heart and mind in the job, then you have no business telling them what their coaching is about.

This is where our holistic view of personal development comes in. Unless we trust the employee to know what they want, how are we going to create people who change first their corner of the company, and then the whole company, and then the world?

The intense focus on individual employees determining their own personal growth goals within a work setting makes the people-centered workplace unique. Cynthia Dyson, head of building support, the communication and consultation branch of the division, put it this way:

> Every employee has to do a personal development plan. Everyone has lofty inspiring goals for themselves and for the path they want to follow. People look at these development plans as more than an opportunity to do some training next month. They actually take it on as, "Where do I see myself in this organization three or five years from now?" They know what potential they possess, and they actually put down on paper their vision for the future: "I want to be there, and I want to be doing this."

I asked three key players in this division how they felt about working in a people-centered workplace:

Dahlie: What is great about this is that we are doing it in an applied sense. This isn't some empty theory; every day we are applying these principles as we work on environmental issues for this company.

We are an energy company. I define energy differently. I look at it as human energy. I actually have not taken a job title. That is a reflection of the working philosophy we have here. I get to try different things all the time. I get to be a witness to people glimpsing their potential. I don't even know what you would call a job like this. I am amazed they pay me for it.

Dyson: It is a nurturing environment in which to grow my leadership skills. I am given the most amazing resources, from coaching to leadership training, to support me in being all I can be. The most exciting thing is that I am starting to see my team helping me grow, as I help them grow.

Balser: I watch us succeed at BC Hydro. We exceed our projections, which makes my boss happy and ensures that the larger company accepts our people-centered workplace. We now have a reputation for delivering the goods in a way that makes the whole company look good. You've got to have that.

We are one of two groups in the company with the highest morale. We are recognized in the company as the place that walks its talk in terms of people development. They trot us out to use as an example.

But much more important, people are taking risks, taking responsibility, and having more authentic conversations than they ever thought they could have at work. And I see people struggling to hold themselves and others accountable for the benefit of the greater good.

This is the only place I know of where we all explicitly hold an enormous vision. It is our ultimate mandate. Nobody imposed it on us. We took it. "To create energy solutions in harmony with the Earth that express the human spirit for our children and for theirs."

This is considerably loftier than BC Hydro's company vision. But that's OK with higher administration because we keep beating our numbers in delivering the goods.

What gives me the greatest satisfaction is that people here will devote their time and energy to saying, "Well, how do we get one step closer to our real vision?" I think that is just immensely wonderful. I wish we could explain to people in other work settings how it can change your life when you are able to commit what you do to some higher purpose.

Conclusion

Webster's defines "to lead" as "to direct, to guide, to direct by influence." Sobriety directs us into leadership moments. By virtue of choosing to be awake, alive, and free from self-imposed stupor or intoxication, we become more reliable and worthy of esteem. Our basic gifts haven't changed. We are still eccentric, or unpredictable, or charming, or wise. But now we are a distilled version of our former addicted self; clearer, more powerful, and more aware of others and ourselves. Now we get to focus that presence for the common good, on some juicy goals that will benefit the world and ourselves.

CHAPTER FOURTEEN

Journey's End

Library Resource Center
Renton Technical College
3000 NE 4th St.
Renton, WA 98056-4195

And what is it to work with love?
It is to weave the cloth with threads drawn from
your heart, even as if your beloved were to wear
that cloth.
It is to build a house with affection, even as if your
beloved were to dwell in that house.
It is to sow seeds with tenderness and reap the harvest with joy, even as if your beloved were to eat
the fruit.
It is to charge all things you fashion with a breath
of your own spirit,
And to know that all the blessed dead are standing
about you and watching....
Work is love made visible.
        —Kahlil Gibran, "On Work," from *The Prophet*

We are at the end of our Working Sober journey. Early
recovery was a process of staying awake and alive day by
day and sometimes second by second. You discovered that
you could hold down a job and stay clean and sober, "with
a little help from your friends."

Or maybe you lost your job and found out that you didn't have to lose your sobriety, too. Maybe you slipped and then learned how to get back on board and stay employed. Your co-workers found out a little about recovery from watching you. You really do not have any idea how many lives you touched just by being able to patch together a recovery that worked.

Then came all those middle-phase recovery issues, like codependency and balancing recovery with everything else important in your life. Settling into your new life and beginning to fashion out of it a life worth living.

And finally those long-term recovery questions began cropping up.

- How do I handle burnout?
- What do I really want to do with my life?
- What about other addictive patterns in my life?
- How do I bridge the gap between recovery and work?
- What am I here on this planet to do?
- Recovery—so what?

These are not questions meant to be easily answered. These are questions that have to be lived. The poet Rainer Maria Rilke describes this process well in *Letters to a Young Poet:*

Have patience with everything unresolved in your heart and try to love the questions themselves as if they were locked rooms or books written in a very foreign language. Don't search for the answers, which could not be given to you now, because you would not be able to live them.

And the point is to live everything. Live the questions now. Perhaps then, someday far in the future, you will gradually, without even knowing it, live your way into the answer.

Through living clean and sober you finally have the capacity to live those tough questions, the ones that make your life meaningful. And in living them, you begin to move from being a taker to being a giver. At work, at home, in meetings, in church, and in your community people begin to look to you for wisdom. You have walked through the dark tunnel of addiction, and, one day at a time, you have made it out into the light.

And now it is time to be of use. To serve others, but not at the expense of yourself. To discover who you truly are through service. Life hands you many venues in which to serve: family, community, the fellowship, and the larger world of politics and big social issues. But service is not something you do every so often. It is something you "be" all the time. And work also asks you to step forward.

In what way shall you be of use to the world? How can you influence those beside you, as you go through your workday? Not by proselytizing or by judging them. But through being fully yourself. The world has been waiting for you to show up. Now that you are here, there is plenty of inspiring work to be done.

We end this Working Sober journey with words about work from Marge Piercy. This poem describes hardworking, passionate, alive people. People like us.

To Be of Use

The people I love the best
jump into work head first
without dallying in the shallows
and swim off with sure strokes almost out of sight.

They seem to become natives of that element,
the black sleek head of seals
bouncing like half submerged balls.

I love people who harness themselves, an ox,
   to a heavy cart,
who pull like water buffalo, with massive patience,
who strain in the mud and the muck
to move things forward,
who do what has to be done, again and again.

I want to be with people who submerge
in the task, who go into the fields to harvest
and work in a row, and pass the bags along,
who are not parlor generals or field deserters
but move in a common rhythm
when the food must come in, or the fire be put out.

The work of the world is common as mud.
Botched, it smears the hands, crumbles to dust.
But the thing worth doing well done
has a shape that satisfies, clean and evident.
Greek amphoras for wine or oil,
Hopi vases that held corn, are put in museums,
but you know they were made to be used.
The pitcher cries for water to carry
and a person for work that is real.

Appendixes

Books as a Recovery Resource

Numerous books about recovery are published every year. They come and they go. Most of the books on this list have been around long enough to weather the test of time. They are written for the recovering person, not for the therapist. The wisdom they contain has helped people for years, and even decades.

Presented in alphabetical order:

Addictive Thinking: Understanding Self-Deception, Abraham J. Twerski, M.D. (Hazelden, 1997). What we call "stinking thinking" in meetings is examined under a microscope in this book. The author looks at all the corners of addictive thinking, from grandiosity to depression. Lots of good case examples and a very readable style make this book a useful tool to help you see how skewed your perspectives might be, and how to choose more healthy ones.

Sample chapters:
- The Addictive Thinker's Concept of Time
- Dealing with Conflict
- Hypersensitivity
- Morbid Expectations
- Must One Reach Bottom?

The Body Betrayed: A Deeper Understanding of Women, Eating Disorders, and Treatment, Kathryn J. Zerbe, M.D. (Gurze Books, 1995). This is an excellent book on eating disorders in women. The author looks at the addictive process within the larger social, historical, and psychological contexts.

One caveat: self-help groups, Twelve Step perspectives, and Overeaters Anonymous are given little attention. All in all it is a rational and readable exploration of this issue.

Sample chapters:

- Daughters and Fathers
- Chasing the Ideal: The Quest for a Perfect Body Image
- Fasting on Love: Concerns about Sexuality and Pregnancy
- Swallowing Anger and Despair: The Impact of Physical and Sexual Abuse
- Drowning Sorrow: Chemical Addictions and Eating Disorders
- Life's Hurdles: Ways Eating Disorders Help Us Cope

Bradshaw On: The Family, John Bradshaw (Health Communications, 1996). Fortunately, and unfortunately, we all come from families. There is a huge readjustment when we need to learn how to cope with our families clean and sober, and they need to learn how to cope with us clean and sober. This book can help.

Bradshaw brought the work of a handful of therapists, psychological system theorists, and addiction treatment specialists to the world. He clearly defines the roles and rules that have trapped many modern families.

Sample chapters:

- The Family as a Rule-Bound System
- Profile of a Functioning Family
- The "Bad" Child: Checklist for How Your Self-Esteem Is Damaged in an Emotionally Abusive Family
- Road Map for Uncovering Your Lost Self: Stage II, Breaking the Spell

Breaking Free: A Recovery Workbook for Facing Codependency, Pia Mellody and Andrea Wells Miller (HarperCollins, 1989). Here is an example of a workbook that is far better than the book on which it's based. The workbook takes each aspect of codependency, defines it clearly, and then gives you exercises that help you see how this symptom plays itself out in your life.

Sample chapters:
- Your History of Abuse
- Step Four
- Setting External Boundaries
- Acknowledging and Meeting Your Own Needs and Wants

Chalk Talk on Alcohol, Father Joseph Martin (Harper-Collins, 1982). Why would anyone read a book by some alcoholic priest talking about his alcoholism in the 1970s? This is still one of the most straightforward, direct books on the nature of this disease. He not only addresses the problems of getting sober, he also faces the problems of staying that way. It is a great read if you are newly in recovery.

Sample chapters:
- The Things We Drink, and Why We Drink Them
- We Don't Have Attitudes, They Have Us
- The Rocky Road to Recovery
- Learning to Love Again

A Gentle Path through the Twelve Steps, Patrick Carnes, Ph.D. (Hazelden, 1994). This is it—the one and only workbook you need for Twelve Step work. You will be writing all over it, and it will become a journal of your journey through the Twelve-Step process. For folks too shy, anxious, or isolated to have a sponsor, this is a great tool to help you see things you might not otherwise discover. For folks with a sponsor, this is a great way to share who you are with him or her.

Sample chapters/tools:
- Family Tree and Addiction
- Loss-of-Reality Inventory
- Personal Craziness Index
- Spiritual Quest Planning Sheet

The Incestuous Workplace: Stress and Distress in the Organizational Family, William L. White (Hazelden, 1997). Prepare to get upset. You will not survive reading this book and still be able to look at your job through the same eyes. It reveals the dark underbelly of the workplace:

> I believe that all organizations are by their very nature conscienceless and essentially predatory. An organization is healthy only to the extent that individuals continue to infuse positive values into it. (page 205)

Yet I finished reading this book feeling hope. He takes an amazingly honest view of what can and can't be done about dysfunctional organizations. His suggestions and perspectives will make you an activist for change wherever you work in the hierarchy.

Sample chapters:
- The Ecology of Professional Stress
- Addiction to Crisis
- The Competition for Strokes
- Gossip and Rumor: Information as Power
- The Abandonment of Elders and the Dilution of Organizational Culture.
- Going Crazy: Is It Me or This Place?

Is It Love or Is It Addiction?, Brenda Schaeffer (Hazelden, 1997). Brenda Schaeffer gives you all the information you would ever want to know about what addictive love looks like, and how it differs from "healthy belonging." She has great stories about love addiction and recovering individuals and couples. The best part of this book is the chapter titled Helping Yourself Out of Love Addiction. Here is a bundle of great exercises for seeing your addictive patterns in relationships and freeing yourself from them.

Sample chapters:
- The Power of Love
- Addictive Lovers
- Power Plays
- From Addiction to Love

Out of the Shadows: Understanding Sexual Addiction, Patrick Carnes, Ph.D. (Hazelden, 1992). When this book came out in 1983 it was the first book to give language to sex addiction. The revised edition is a great resource for sex addicts. Carnes is able to clearly and simply discuss both the uniqueness of sexual addictions and their commonality with other addictive patterns.

Sample chapters:
- The Addictive Cycle
- The Family and the Addict's World
- The Future Is Conditional

Second-Year Sobriety: Getting Comfortable Now That Everything Is Different and *Third-Year Sobriety: Finding Out Who You Really Are*, Guy Kettelhack (Hazelden, 1998). Finally some books about later-stage recovery. These books are very readable, liberally sprinkled with life stories of recovering folks. For example, the author takes a hard look at such issues as feelings of entitlement, loneliness, cleaning up wreckage, hunger for high drama, sponsorship, over-doing it, sex, love, food, and perfectionism.

Sample chapters from *Second-Year Sobriety:*
- Discovering What's Normal for You
- Emotional Storms: From Danger to Self-Discovery

Sample chapters from *Third-Year Sobriety:*
- Being Open, Setting Boundaries
- What Does the Program Mean to Me Now?
- Dealing with Other Addictive Behaviors

Seven Weeks to Sobriety, Joan Mathews Larson, Ph.D. (Ballantine Wellspring, 1997). This is a great resource for understanding the connection between diet and relapse. The author is a bit messianic about nutrition as the cure for addictions. But there is no question in my mind that diet can help reduce the threat of relapse and that using nutritional supplements can ease the painful transition from using to being sober. Just be sure to add one large grain of salt to her recommendations.

Sample chapters:
- It's Not All in Your Mind
- Week 3: Correcting Chemistry
- Week 5: Goodbye, Depression
- Week 6: Biochemical Traps That Block Recovery

Under the Influence, James Milam and Katherine Ketcham (Bantam Books, 1983). This is the book to give family and friends to help them understand what an addiction is. It is the clearest presentation of the disease model of alcoholism.

Sample chapters:
- What Makes an Alcoholic: Predisposing Factors
- Getting the Alcoholic into Treatment

- Beyond Prejudice and Misconception
- Medications Containing Alcohol
- Guidelines for a Hypoglycemic Diet

A Woman's Way through the Twelve Steps, Stephanie S. Covington, Ph.D. (Hazelden, 1994). I would never have come in contact with this book if my editor hadn't said, "You've got to read this!" It is misnamed! I got so much good advice and solace from it. True, some chapters like the chapter on the Forth Step should be required reading for all recovering women. But many of the ways of seeing recovery, like the chapter on Step Nine, are as true for me as for any woman. As the genders start coming together, this book becomes more relevant to all of us.

Sample chapters:
- Are We Really Powerless?
- Creating a Personal Image of God
- Taking "Wrongs" Too Literally
- Humility Not Humiliation
- Putting the Day To Bed

Women, Sex, and Addiction, Charlotte Davis Kasl (HarperCollinsw, 1990). This book was written for women recovering from a sexual addiction. Yet her insights apply equally to any woman in recovery, and in fact to all of us raised in this sexually confused culture. She addresses both the addiction and the codependency that contaminates intimacy.

Sample chapters:
- The Nature of Addiction: Seeing the Body but Not the Soul
- From Grace Kelly to Prostitution: How Sexual Addiction and Codependency Intertwine

- Anything to Fill Up This Emptiness: One Addiction or Many?
- How Did I Get This Way? Culture, Family, and the Grace of God

The World Wide Web as a Recovery Resource

The Internet provides an entirely new support system for recovering addicts and alcoholics. It also provides some pitfalls to recovery. Replacing an addiction to substances with an addiction to the World Wide Web is not necessarily progress.

Internet Addiction

How can you tell when an activity has turned the corner from a pleasurable one to an addictive one? One guideline is to track how much of your daily life is taken up with doing the activity or planning to do it. A heroin junkie spends relatively little time shooting, but a lot of time scoring the dope and getting ready for or recovering from the act.

A rich life is lived in balance. If your professional, family, community, or personal life is suffering from your focus on this activity, then it's time to get curious and start inquiring whether you may have become addicted. I became inadvertently addicted to computer games for a while, until I recognized the addictive patterns and how they paralleled my alcoholism. It was affecting my relationship with my wife and my daughter. I was thinking about the game even when I wasn't playing it. I realized that I had to set computer games aside.

Some people get addicted to Internet surfing. Some get addicted to chat rooms. Most do not: they find enjoyment in the computer without having it begin to possess their lives. Look under "Primary Sites, Internet Addiction" below for a resource for this pattern of behavior.

Web Sites for Recovery

The Internet is a madhouse: sites coming and going, technology always changing—3-D, streaming videos, sites that track you down. The hot recovery resource this month may be out of date by the next.

I broke down this section into two subsections: primary sites and resource hubs. An example of a primary site is the home page for Alcoholics Anonymous. An example of a resource hub is "The Web of Addictions," a site with lots of links to other sites, as well as links to current addiction-related articles. I am using two conventions in listing the URL, the site address. I am enclosing the address in parentheses (www.workingsober.com), but in actually using the address you would not include the parentheses. And I am leaving off the prefix address http://, which must come ahead of every address.

Primary Sites

Alcoholics Anonymous (www.alcoholics-anonymous.org/econtent.html): This takes you to an index page for the site. Here are links for the newly recovering, teens, media, professionals using AA as a resource, information about upcoming conventions, and the *A.A. Grapevine*. This site provides a solid introduction to what AA is all about.

Narcotics Anonymous (www.na.org): A home page with news, help for professionals, basic information about the organization, and group registration sections. It is not as user-friendly to a newcomer as the AA page is.

Overeaters Anonymous (www.overeaters.org): Good sections addressing the question "Is OA for you?" and the perspective of the health care professional. The meeting locator button is a joke; it only relates to intergroups in Minnesota, and otherwise dumps you into an e-mail address of someone who can refer you to a local meeting.

Gamblers Anonymous (www.gamblersanonymous.org/index. html) has pages on its history, the Twelve Steps, a self-test, some questions and answers, and some Gam-anon information for family and friends.

Debtors Anonymous (www.debtorsanonymous.org): Check out the fact sheet page (www.debtorsanonymous.org/ fact.html) for the heart of the information about this organization and for tools, history, a test, meeting format, and information for professionals and media.

Sex Addicts Anonymous (www.sexaa.org): Some material to help with the question "Are you a sex addict?" as well as information about the program and an online store for literature. There is no adequate official site for SLAA, just a page with a mailing address and phone number on it. But check out these private sites:

- (www.geocities.com/hotsprings/villa/1913)—an unofficial SLAA site
- (www.sexaddictionhelp.com)—run by a treatment center in Houston and a site with many resources, free and not, as well as a good self-assessment tool
- (www.ncsac.org)—the home page for the National Council on Sexual Addiction and Compulsivity, with lots of solid information about this addiction

Internet Addiction (netaddiction.com): This site deals with cybersex addictions, cyberaffairs, and compulsive on-line gambling, auctioning, and day-trading. If you are beginning to wonder about your computer habit, check out the test at (www.netaddiction.com/resources/test.htm). This site is run by a private, nonprofit health care company and is not a fellowship. But it is worth checking out.

Al-Anon and Alateen (www.al-anon-alateen.org/eng.index. html): Lots of twenty-question self-assessments for adults, teens, and adult children of alcoholics. Everything you could want to know about Al-Anon. No pages for mental health professionals or media, however.

Codependents Anonymous (CoDA) (www.codependents.org): This is a very well done site, about twenty pages deep. The index has pages well sorted by categories like tools for recovery, meetings/sharing, literature, and news and events. It is very participatory, encouraging CoDA members to add to the site.

Looking for a meeting in your hometown or in London? Check out these next two resources:

12stepmeetings.com (12stepmeetings.com/index.html): A very cool service acting as an unofficial collection of information about many Twelve Step groups both nationally and internationally, including on-line meetings.

United Way "First Call for Help" Lines: This service, funded by United Way will give you information about almost every self-help group in your area. When I tried it for the San Francisco Bay Area, it took a couple of minutes to get through. They told me that they would give me the number of local fellowship or intergroup offices, but they did not have information about specific meetings. This is a very large catchment district, so that was understandable. There is a limited geographic coverage for this service (only one number for Alaska, for instance), but to download a directory of these useful numbers go to (www.geocities.com/hotsprings/villa/1913/firstcallforhelp.html).

Secular Organizations for Sobriety (SOS)
(www.secularhumanism.org/sos) is the nonspiritual recovery program. It fills the need for fellowship for folks who just can't handle the God talk in Twelve Step meetings. This site will tell you everything you need to know about this organization.

Hazelden Foundation: (www.hazelden.org) features a wide range of online resources for recovering individuals, their families, and professionals, including an extensive online bookstore, free recovery tools such as daily meditations and electronic greetings, "e-community" activities like chat and bulletin boards, online author events, regular newsletters, information on all Hazelden inpatient and outpatient treatment services, general recovery resources, quizzes, and regularly updated information, as well as extensive professional resource links and research libraries.

Working Sober (www.workingsober.com) is the official site for information about recovery in the workplace. It has sections of this book available to share with co-workers, Working Sober accessories, "Ask Skibbins" advice corner, and a place where you can share your work-setting recovery story with the author and perhaps become a part of *Working Sober 2: The Sequel.*

Resource Hubs

Sobriety and Recovery Resources (www.recoveryresources.org): Here are hundreds of links to recovery-based sites. This is the most updated hub, yet even here you will run into many "This page not available" messages. That is the ever-changing nature of the Web.

Web of Addictions (www.well.com/user/woa/index.html): This was the first award-winning recovery-based hub. It contains fact sheets on drugs, links, meetings, topics, and the latest research. Launched in 1995, many of its links are now out of service, but it still is a good resource.

Grant Me the Serenity (www.open-mind.org): My favorite hub, this has all sorts of interesting links, and is annotated so you know what to expect when you link out. It has Twelve Step and support groups that I had never encountered before, including Lip Balm Anonymous (for real!) and Media Anonymous for help in recovering from media dependency. Be sure to check out the Recovery Medicine Wheel.

Workbook Pages

Chapter 1: Your First Week Back

(See chapter 1 for background and for examples of these activities.)

1–1. Tool #1: Two Times Five Equals AOK

Simple Instruction #1: Make *two* support calls *every day* while at work. Not big complicated calls. Not long protracted calls. Simple calls. Calls *one to five* minutes long. If you get an answering machine, just leave a message. Do this every workday for the first month. Fill out the chart.

Call Checklist

	Call #1	Call #2
Monday	_____	_____
Tuesday	_____	_____
Wednesday	_____	_____
Thursday	_____	_____
Friday	_____	_____
Monday	_____	_____
Tuesday	_____	_____
Wednesday	_____	_____
Thursday	_____	_____
Friday	_____	_____

	Call #1	Call #2
Monday	_____	_____
Tuesday	_____	_____
Wednesday	_____	_____
Thursday	_____	_____
Friday	_____	_____
Monday	_____	_____
Tuesday	_____	_____
Wednesday	_____	_____
Thursday	_____	_____
Friday	_____	_____
Monday	_____	_____
Tuesday	_____	_____
Wednesday	_____	_____
Thursday	_____	_____
Friday	_____	_____
Monday	_____	_____
Tuesday	_____	_____
Wednesday	_____	_____
Thursday	_____	_____
Friday	_____	_____
Monday	_____	_____
Tuesday	_____	_____
Wednesday	_____	_____
Thursday	_____	_____
Friday	_____	_____

1–2. The Holmes and Rahe Stress Test

Life Changes: Add up the score of the changes that have happened to you in the past year.

___ Death of a spouse: 100

___ Divorce: 73

___ Relapse from recovery: 67

___ Marital separation: 65

___ Detention in jail or institution: 63

___ Death of a close family member: 63

___ Addictive behavior: 60

___ Major personal injury or illness: 53

___ Marriage: 50

___ Going into recovery: 48

___ Being fired at work: 47

___ Marital reconciliation: 45

___ Retirement: 45

___ Major change in health or behavior of a family member: . 44

___ Pregnancy: 40

___ Sexual difficulty: 40

___ Gaining a new family member through birth,
adoption, or remarriage: 39

___ Major business readjustments: 39

___ Major change in financial state: 38

___ Death of a close friend: 37

___ Change to a different line of work: 36

___ Major increase in fights with spouse: 35

___ Taking on a mortgage: 31

___ Foreclosure on a mortgage or loan: 30

___ Major change in responsibility at work: 29

___ Son or daughter leaving home: 29

___ In-law troubles: 29

___ Outstanding personal achievement: 28

___ Spouse begins to cease work outside of home: 26

___ Going back to school: 26

___ Major change in living condition (rebuilding, remodeling): 25

___ Revision of personal habits: 24

___ Troubles with superior, boss: 23

___ Major change in working hours, conditions: 20

___ Change in residence: 20

___ Change to a new school: 20

___ Major change in usual type and/or amount of recreation: 19

___ Major change in church activities: 19

___ Major change in social activities: 18

___ Purchasing a new car, or other big purchase: 17

___ Major change in sleeping habits: 16

___ Major change in number of family get-togethers: 15

___ Major change in eating habits: 15

___ Vacation: 13

___ Christmas or holiday observance: 12

___ Minor violations of the law: 11

Add up your total Life Change Units (your LCUs).

Total LCU below 150: . . . . 35 percent chance of illness or
accident within two years

Total LCU between 150 and 300: 51 percent chance of illness or
accident

Total LCU over 300: . . . . 80 percent chance of illness or
accident

1–3. Tool #3: S.T.O.P

You can put this sign on your desk where you can see it in an emergency.

If your co-workers are dumping on you remember: (1) smile; (2) Stop Talking—*they are* Obviously Projecting; (3) apologize; and (4) get out of Dodge. You are in no condition to do anything more subtle than that.

If you want to dump on them remember: "Stop Talking—*I am* Obviously Projecting." Smile, and create some real distance between the two of you in a hurry. Quickly, before you really blow it.

1–4. Tool #5: The Four Directions

Direction #1—Stay clean and sober. Go to meetings, call therapists, sponsors, coaches, and suicide-prevention hotlines; call anyone for help instead of going back to drinking or drugging.

Direction #2—Survive. Sleep as best as you can, eat as best as you can, and take at least one slow walk a day, if you can.

Direction #3—Try to physically show up on your job. Forget showing up intellectually, or energetically—that will come in time. Just try to get your body there.

Direction #4—Go back to Direction #1.

This week, if it is not direction #1, 2, 3 or 4, avoid it.

1–5. Checklist for Hard Weeks

- Get lots of help.
- Avoid slippery places.
- Keep your distance from angry and critical people.
- That includes you.
- Remember to call someone supportive twice a day.
- Get the flu.
- S.T.O.P.
- Send your Inner Judge on vacation.
- Follow the Four Directions.

Chapter 2: I Didn't Go to Treatment, I Just Started AA/NA

2–1. Surrender at Work

Let them help: Give up having to be the expert. Learn how to ask others for their ideas about how to make something work more effectively. Ask for help. Solicit advice from everyone, customers included. Delegate; learn how to turn work over to others. It is always easier at first just to "do it yourself." But by being patient, and allowing others to do a less than perfect job, you empower them and reduce your own workload.

Red light, green light: Pay attention to meaningful coincidences at work, and accept that they may be pointing you in a particular direction. If a project or task is moving forward effortlessly, that may be a signal that it is in accordance with the unfolding of the universe. If something is continually crashing and burning, that may be a signal that something is out of balance.

Calling Upstairs: Listen with your whole body. Here are three approaches for gaining closer contact with that knowing:

1. Space in your day. Create space in your day when you can be quiet enough to listen to the whisperings of your inner wisdom. You need some privacy and some quiet. You must consciously carve out a little time for this; for example, by sitting still and silent for five minutes in the morning, or taking a slow, solitary lunchtime walk or an after-dinner stroll, or simply reflecting on your day before falling asleep.

2. Knowing what to ask for. Become willing to ask for help for anything and everything. And be content with what you get. Often it will be no answer at all. That is an answer, too.

3. Is it real or is it Memorex?
   - Sense your body. If you feel muscles in your stomach or chest, or anywhere in your body contracting, hardening, or getting anxious, begin to wonder if this is really a message from your Higher Power. Generally (although not always) there is a feeling of relaxation that comes with true intuition.
   - Listen to the message. Your Higher Power sees you as naturally resourceful, wise, creative, and whole. Its guidance supports your health and well-being. If the message is harsh, judgmental, or subtly implies that you are deficient, stupid, stuck, or a mess, then begin to wonder if it might be an impostor.
   - Don't blindly trust any inner voice. You may get a dazzling insight, with a huge relaxation, and a deep inner knowing that this is the truth. And that

insight might be saying, "Now you can recreationally use alcohol and other drugs!" Sit still with any
message, and see if it fits into the way you want to
live your life. Many of us in early recovery have
gotten great ideas to quit our jobs, dump our partners, reject our parents, and head off to Alaska.
Some of those ideas may, in the long run, turn out
to be OK. Some may be the fast lane to disaster.
The grander the plan, the longer you need to just
sit with it and see if it looks that good a week or a
month from now. True guidance will endure.

Chapter 3: Your Relapse Prevention Tool Kit

3–1. Tool #1: It Pays to Advertise

Post discreet signs around your workplace.

> **Call first**

Call someone outside work and bounce your reactions off
them before making a mess!

> **Stay curious**

Remember, you don't really know what other people are
thinking! Don't assume they're judging you.

> **Look before you leap...**

down their throats.

> **Now + 5**

Take five minutes before overreacting!

> **Be aware of success**

Beware, sudden success can leave you in an upbeat, excited state that can lead to unexpected relapse.

Make up your own signs. Pictures, too. You might choose peaceful scenes that remind you of that place of serenity inside you. Be creative, and surround your workplace with recovery reminders that only you fully understand.

3–2. Tool #2: The Craving Deconstructor

Relapse Crave Process:
Stimulus → Craving → Plan → Action: drinking/using

Recovery Crave Deconstructor:
Stimulus → Craving → Plan → /// Interrupt action: refocus on recovery

Before recovery, the planning stage was an instantaneous and unconscious stage. In recovery, this is the place to wedge in the Craving Deconstructor and break the relapse craving cycle. The trick is to wake up in the middle of planning how to get loaded. Here are three of ways to derail the crave, by slowing down the planning phase.

The Keys to the Kingdom. Put your car keys in a screw-top jar at home or in a zippered case at work. Say a phrase that expresses your feeling of gratitude whenever you open the case or jar to use the keys: "Thank God I am sober today."

Or "No more hangovers." Or "I know what I did last night." Or whatever phrase that best expresses your relief at being sober.

The Phone is Now Your Friend. You found out how to use ads in Tool #1. The first ad needs to go on top of all your phones, at home, cell phone, and at work.

> ### Stay Awake!

Home, James. This is another ad. Put it in your car.

> ### Home, James!

When you see it, think of the best things you can about home. It may be the quiet or the connection with someone else, the privacy or the friendly chaos. Replace any relapse plan with an image of your home as a refuge. And go straight home.

3–3. Tool #3: Drawing the Cloak

1. Find a comfortable place and read the following visualization.

Settle into a comfortable position. Good. Now just pay attention to your breath. Feel your chest rising and falling as the air comes in and out. If you notice your mind wanting to grab your attention away from your breath, just sigh, and ask your brain to leave you alone for a little while, and return your focus to your breath. In and out. Gentle. Good. Feel yourself settling down into your breath, and relaxing a little more each time you exhale.

Now imagine that there is a movie screen inside

your mind, which right now is gray, as you breathe in and out. Gradually the screen begins to light up, and you see an image of a place in your life when you were very peaceful, quiet, and content. See the picture of what was around you, and hear the sounds, smell the smells, feel yourself back in that comfortable, calm, serene place. You are there in the movie, just relaxing and enjoying the tranquil mood.

In front of you is an old chest. Look closely at it. It is locked with an ancient iron lock, but you notice that you have the key in your pocket. You open the lock, and then you open the chest.

You find several objects inside. Pick each one up and examine it. You may be surprised at what you find. If you see nothing, just make something up. All these gifts are yours. Each one will support your recovery. Spend some time getting to know each object.

Finally, in the bottom of the chest there is a cloak. Pull it out and hold it up to look at it. It is beautiful. Take a moment to enjoy how it looks. Now wrap it around your shoulders. It fits you perfectly. As you feel the weight and texture of it, you discover that it is a magic cloak. It has absorbed the stillness, restfulness, and serenity of this place. You know that, whenever you wrap it around you, you will be back in this place, and you will feel the gentleness of this moment.

Each of these gifts is magical. Find a place inside you where you can store each one for the time when you need it. Then close the chest, and again become aware of your breath. As you breathe in and out, the movie screen begins to fade back into gray. You are aware of your body. You feel comfortable and rested.

You remember the gifts you brought back with you, and you understand how they can support your recovery. You open your eyes.

2. Take some time to write down your experience. If you have some crayons or colored pens, draw your cloak. If you don't have any art supplies, consider getting some.

---

3. Use the cloak. Walk outside or go the rest room, back stairs, or storage closet, or somewhere where you can be alone. Remember your cloak, and wrap it around you. Breathe in the calmness and the quiet. Feel your inner core begin to settle and relax. Stay there a little longer than you think you should. Then wrap your cloak up and put it in its safe place inside you.

3–4. Tool #4: Gold Stamps

Copy these onto gold-colored paper and collect them.

3–5. Tool #5: The Denial Destroyer

The BS Detector: On a three-by-five-inch card, write down all the lies your Inner Addict tells you about drinking and using. Now take this card, and read each lie out loud. After you read each one, say the ritual phrase, "No, that is a lie!" If you don't fully believe that the statement is a lie, keep repeating, "No, that is a lie!" even though you are arguing with yourself. After a while you may let yourself see the truth. If you can't get past one, start making some phone calls to your support people, and talk with them about it. Stay with that statement until you know the statement is a trick and is false. Only when you can say with vehemence, "No, that is a lie!" can you go on to the next one.

When you have finished all the statements, set fire to the card and burn it up entirely. No more lies. From now on when the Inner Addict tries to talk you into breaking your sobriety by telling you one of these lies, you will simply say, "No, that is a lie."

The Truth Record: To make this tool, pick up another three-by-five card. On one side write down a list of the trials, struggles, and messes that resulted from your drinking or drug taking; just the highlights (or lowlights) of the worst moments. Use just a few words so that you remember.

On the other side of the card, list the best of the good

things that have come to you since recovery. This card is a record of the truth about your sobriety and about what came before. Always carry it with you. Add to it when you need to. Anytime you begin to feel that using might be a swell idea, just pull it out and read both sides. The truth shall set you free.

Chapter 4: Managing Anger: The Four C's

(See chapter 4 for background information.)

4–1. Chill Cheater

- "Can I get back to you about that?"
- "I can see that you are upset, and I'll think about what you said."
- "This isn't a good time to talk; let's do lunch!" (a southern California approach)
- "I want to respond, but I can't right now."
- "I have to go, I can't talk right now."
- "The boss wants to see me; we'll have to talk later."
- Your favorites:

_____

_____

_____

_____

4–2. Tool #1: Anger Channels

- Tear up old phone books.
- Smash glass into the recycling containers.
- Roll up the windows of your car and scream.
- Hit the bed with a small baseball bat.
- Throw rocks against a wall.

- Work out vigorously.
- Take it out on a punching bag.
- Rip up old rags.
- Run or walk very hard.
- Climb the stairs in your building as fast as you can.
- Your favorites:

_____

_____

_____

_____

4–3. Tool #2: Cleaning the Slate

You will need

- a trained receiver
- four to five minutes in a place where you can raise your voice and say everything you need to say
- a willingness to move beyond cleaning the slate once you finish

Rules for Receivers

1. Encourage the blurting out of all the junk that needs to be released. Match the clearer's intensity by using comments like the following:

- "Yeah!"
- "That's right!"
- "That sounds horrible!"
- "Tell me some more about that."
- "Bummer!"
- "That must have made you mad!"
- "What else is in there?"

2. Keep time, not more than five minutes.

3. Do not join the Clearer in assassinating the character of the Clearer's target.

4. Do not judge the Clearer or give advice.

5. Help the Clearer move to the next stage. Ask the Clearer what he or she intends to do next about the situation. "So, now what do you want to do about it?" Just ask that question. Do not advise, comment on the plan, or tell the Clearer the right thing to do. Just wish the Clearer well.

4–4. Tool #3: The Ladder

1. "I know we have a problem here. Would you agree to talk about it with me?

2. "If I could talk first, I just want to tell you what I saw and ask a few questions about it. Then you can respond. Will that work?" (If not, then let the other person speak first. Don't respond or react, just listen. When it is your turn, go to number 3.)

3. "I want to share what I heard you say to me when we were arguing." Share just the words and details as you remember them from the conflict, with no interpretations.

4. Then say, "And this is the story I made up about what happened." Now share how you interpreted what the other said or did.

5. Then say, "I want to check out what was really going on with you." Then listen.

6. If no real dialogue is happening from this interaction, or if you start getting too defensive and explosive, or if you

feel the other person is just out to make you suffer, you may need to back away from this. Thank him or her for talking with you and get away before exploding.

4–5. Tool #4: Vengeance Exercise
Answer items 1 and 2 before you turn the page.

1. List ten times when you really blew up.

    1. _____

    2. _____

    3. _____

    4. _____

    5. _____

    6. _____

    7. _____

    8. _____

    9. _____

  10. _____

2. List five times when you held your temper in and didn't attack the other person.

    1. _____

    2. _____

    3. _____

    4. _____

    5. _____

3. Now write down what the long-term results of those actions were.

When my anger exploded:

1. _____

2. _____

3. _____

4. _____

5. _____

6. _____

7. _____

8. _____

9. _____

10. _____

When I held anger in check:

1. _____

2. _____

3. _____

4. _____

5. _____

Is vengeance and explosive drama worth it?

Chapter 5: Out of Work

(See chapter 5 for background and examples.)

5–1. Tool #1: Values Clarification

We are going to make a list of your core values. First write out the answers to the following questions:

1. Think of a time when your life was great. The world appreciated what you had to bring it. Paint that time in your mind's eye. Now look at what values were being honored by others at that time. What qualities that you possess were being seen by your world?

2. Now think of a time when you were angry and upset. Pick a time when someone was walking all over you. Which of your values were being disrespected in that moment?

3. What makes you feel like your life is a success? If you notice that there are things (a Rolex, a Saab convertible) that make you feel successful, what do those thing say about you? What values emerge when you look here?

4. What would make your life totally fulfilling?

5. What is most important to you?

6. What are some things your friends know about you that you might not even include on a list of values, because they are so apparent to you?

Now, from your written answers start pulling out a list of at least ten core values. Other ones may pop up. Include them on your list. This can be quite a long list.

My Values

	Five Core Values (Prioritize 1–5)	How much in my life? (On a scale of 1–10)	Visual Image
1.			
2.			
3.			
4.			
5.			
6.			
7.			
8.			
9.			
10.			

List more, if you wish.

_____

_____

_____

_____

_____

_____

_____

_____

_____

Five Core Values (Prioritize 1–5)	How much in my life? (On a scale of 1–10)	Visual Image

Write your values in the first column, placing the most important value in the blank for number 1 and so on. In the next column, rate each of the values you listed in terms of how extensively you live them. A score of 1 or 2 means you just think you should live that value and you intend to get around to it someday. A score of 9 or 10 means you live that value every day and that you couldn't imagine living any other way. In the last column, draw a picture that captures the essence of each of your values.

Chapter 8: The Balancing Act

(See chapter 8 for background and examples.)

8–1. Tool #1: Perspective Work

Fill in the blank spaces with your perspectives, the things you tell yourself about time. Some of them may be limiting beliefs you have about time. Make sure to include positive perspectives that you may hold, or may want to hold. Maybe a brand-new perspective on time might pop up. If your list goes to nine or ten, that's fine.

Perspectives on Time

Perspective	How it feels to be inside it
1.	
2.	
3.	
4.	
5.	
6.	
7.	
8.	
9.	
10.	

Write next to each perspective how it feels when you are standing inside it. How does the world look from that perspective? Do you like it? Is it confining? What comes up for you when you are seeing the world from those eyes?

Choose the perspective that will bring you the most aliveness.

Imagine a new perspective. Write about what it would be like to live from this perspective.

_____

_____

_____

_____

_____

_____

_____

_____

_____

_____

_____

_____

_____

_____

_____

_____

_____

_____

_____

_____

_____

8–2. My Yes and No List

If I say "Yes!" to	Then I will have to say "No!" to

Chapter 10: Dare to Dream Again

(See chapter 10 for background and examples.)

10–1. Tool: The Belief Deconstructor

List all the bad things you are saying about yourself.

1. _____

2. _____

3. _____

4. _____

5. _____

6. _____

7. _____

8. _____

9. _____

For each accusation above, write a retraction; state the truth about each.

1. _____

2. _____

3. _____

4. _____

5. _____

6. _____

7. _____

8. _____

9. _____

10–2. Writing Your Vision Statement

1. Determine the territory.
   - recovery
   - your physical body (health, fitness, appearance)
   - your environment (home, office, car)
   - your relationships (family, lover, life partner, work, church, community, old friends, and others)
   - your spiritual or philosophical life (your source of meaning)
   - your personal growth and mental health
   - your career (vocation, money management, retirement)
   - your recreational life

   Customize this list to fit the important areas of your life

2. Step into the future.

   Begin by feeling your breath. Watch as it slows and deepens. Follow your breath as you draw it into your lungs. Imagine you draw it deeper and deeper into your belly with each breath....

   Now imagine the television set of your mind gently glowing. As you look closer you can see that it is a new program called "This Will Be Your Life." You see that this show is about you, ten years from now. It begins with some scenes from your early years. Notice which scenes come on the screen....Then it shows you as you are this year. Again see what important images from the past twelve months come on the screen.... Now it cuts to a scene of you ten years from now, speaking directly to you today. Your future self is telling you today about what your life is like, what you do for money, whom you are with, where you live, and what you do with your time. Listen and watch carefully as your future self shows you scenes of your life ten years hence…. Now the show is over, and the glow dies, and you return to an awareness of your breath and your body. You are awakening refreshed and aware of everything you saw and heard.

Write down your experience. Now, from your list and from your experience in front of your internal TV, begin to write your vision.

3. Write your vision.
   - Write as though it has already happened. In this way it pulls you toward it.
   - Don't pull your punches.
   - Be specific. State ambitious goals that you can measure and be proud of.
   - Include all areas of your life.
   - Tell yourself "for the sake of what." State what your purpose on this planet in this lifetime is all about. Be bold.

10–3. Planning Worksheet

Planning for the month of _____
Visionary goal: _____

List the projects that need to be accomplished to meet that goal, with completion date:

1. _____

2. _____

3. _____

4. _____

5. _____

This month's target for each of these projects, with completion date:

1. _____

2. _____

3. _____

4. _____

5. _____

On the first of each month, schedule into your daily planner time to work on projects.

Chapter 11: What about the Rest of Us?

11–1. Tool #1: Sane Exercise Record

Sane Exercise Record

Each day log how many minutes you did some
simple exercise: walking, stairclimbing, hiking, and so on

Month: _May_ Week: 1__ 2_X_3__ 4__ 5__ Comments: _I did it!_

	10 min.	15 min.	20 min.	25 min.	30 min.
Monday	12				
Tuesday	5				
Wednesday		16			
Thursday	10				
Friday			22 Yea!		
Saturday		14			
Sunday	10				

11–2. Tool #3: Disentangling

(See chapter 11 for an example.)

Write down a belief that you think is getting in your way. Try to distinguish between the surface belief and the hidden belief underlying it. Write them in the spaces provided. Beneath each of those, write what you know to be true about the belief.

Original Belief:

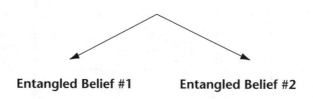

Entangled Belief #1   **Entangled Belief #2**

_____

Lesson:

Chapter 12: The Twelve Steps for Managers and Leaders

12–1. A Management Fourth Step

Questions about Power and Control

1. Under what conditions do I demand obedience?

2. How am I feeling about the people I supervise in those moments when I demand obedience from them?

3. Who demanded obedience from me when I was a child, and how did that affect me?

4. Who demands my obedience now, and how does that make me feel?

5. What makes me feel out of control at work, and what do I do about it?

6. Examine your relationship with each person you supervise. One by one, look at the way you have used or abused power and control in your relationship with that person.

Questions about Image Management

1. What characteristics, talents, behaviors, and attitudes do I want my co-workers and supervisors to admire in me?

2. What do I need to hide about myself in order to win their admiration?

3. What else am I afraid to show others about myself?

4. What aspects of those people I supervise repel me?

5. What do I do to make sure they don't show their truth to me?

6. How much of my time and life energy do I spend presenting a false mask at work? How often am I genuine, authentic, open, and honest about my truth?

Questions about Obsession with Profit

1. What is my most truthful definition of profit?

2. What do I sacrifice in my life (for example, time, relationships, energy, rest, quality of life) in order to increase my company's profit?

3. What do I expect those people I supervise to sacrifice in order to make the company more profitable and to protect my job?

4. Open your daily planner. Divide last week into half-hour time slots, so that you have 48 time slots a day, 336 slots for the week. Count how many of these 336 slots you spent participating in each of the following activities and put that number next to the listed category.

	Activity	Number of Slots
Profit-related:	work and work-related activities:	
Not for profit:	intimate relationship:	
	parenting:	
	other home/family-related activities:	
	friends:	
	community activities:	
	church-related activities:	
	recovery-related activities:	

Activity   **Number of Slots**

sleep:

eating:

health-related activities:

active recreation (hiking, tennis, etc.):

passive recreation (TV, computer):

other:

What do you notice about your choices?

The Twelve Steps of Alcoholics Anonymous

1. We admitted we were powerless over alcohol—that our lives had become unmanageable.

2. Came to believe that a Power greater than ourselves could restore us to sanity.

3. Made a decision to turn our will and our lives over to the care of God *as we understood Him.*

4. Made a searching and fearless moral inventory of ourselves.

5. Admitted to God, to ourselves, and to another human being the exact nature of our wrongs.

6. Were entirely ready to have God remove all these defects of character.

7. Humbly asked Him to remove our shortcomings.

8. Made a list of all persons we had harmed, and became willing to make amends to them all.

9. Made direct amends to such people wherever possible, except when to do so would injure them or others.

10. Continued to take personal inventory and when we were wrong promptly admitted it.

The Twelve Steps of AA are taken from *Alcoholics Anonymous,* 3d ed., published by AA World Services, Inc., New York, N.Y., 59–60. Reprinted with permission of AA World Services, Inc. (See editor's note on copyright page.)

11. Sought through prayer and meditation to improve our conscious contact with God *as we understood Him,* praying only for knowledge of His will for us and the power to carry that out.

12. Having had a spiritual awakening as the result of these steps, we tried to carry this message to alcoholics, and to practice these principles in all our affairs.

Index

About the Author

David Skibbins, Ph.D., P.C.C.P., has been in clinical practice for twenty-five years and has done psychotherapy with addicted clients for seventeen years. He is a certified professional life coach. He has taught undergraduate courses in addiction treatment, psychotherapy, and psychological assessment for the past fifteen years.

He received his bachelor's and master's degrees from John F. Kennedy University and his doctorate degree from The Professional School of Psychology. He is a member of the National Association of Alcoholism and Drug Abuse Counselors and the Employee Assistance Professionals Association.

Hazelden Information and Educational Services is a division of the Hazelden Foundation, a not-for-profit organization. Since 1949, Hazelden has been a leader in promoting the dignity and treatment of people afflicted with the disease of chemical dependency.

The mission of the foundation is to improve the quality of life for individuals, families, and communities by providing a national continuum of information, education, and recovery services that are widely accessible; to advance the field through research and training; and to improve our quality and effectiveness through continuous improvement and innovation.

Stemming from that, the mission of this division is to provide quality information and support to people wherever they may be in their personal journey—from education and early intervention, through treatment and recovery, to personal and spiritual growth.

Although our treatment programs do not necessarily use everything Hazelden publishes, our bibliotherapeutic materials support our mission and the Twelve Step philosophy upon which it is based. We encourage your comments and feedback.

The headquarters of the Hazelden Foundation are in Center City, Minnesota. Additional treatment facilities are located in Chicago, Illinois; New York, New York; Plymouth, Minnesota; St. Paul, Minnesota; and West Palm Beach, Florida. At these sites, we provide a continuum of care for men and women of all ages. Our Plymouth facility is designed specifically for youth and families.

For more information on Hazelden, please call **1-800-257-7800**. Or you may access our World Wide Web site on the Internet at **www.hazelden.org**.